THY STRONG WORD

The Enduring Legacy of Martin Franzmann

RICHARD N. BRINKLEY

Foreword by Carl F. Schalk

Publishing House
St. Louis

Martin Hans Franzmann (1907–76)

This book is dedicated to my wife, Carolyn, and to my children, Jonathan, Katherine, Lydia, and Johanna. May they continue to sing the Lord's song throughout their lives.

Copyright © 1993 Concordia Publishing House
3558 S. Jefferson Avenue, St. Louis, MO 63118-3968
Manufactured in the United States of America

Library of Congress Cataloging-in-Publication Data

Brinkley, Richard N., 1950—
    Thy strong word : the enduring legacy of Martin Franzmann / Richard N. Brinkley.
       p.   cm.
    Includes bibliographical references and index.
    ISBN 0-570-01347-X
    1. Franzmann, Martin H. 2. Hymn writers—United States—Biography. 3. Lutheran Church—Hymns—History and criticism. 4. Lutheran Church—Missouri Synod—Hymns—History and criticism. 5. Hymns, English—United States—History and criticism. I. Title.
BV330.F65B75 1993
264'.2'092—dc20   93-28284
[B]   CIP

1   2   3   4   5   6   7   8   9   10   02   01   00   99   98   97   96   95   94   93

ACKNOWLEDGMENTS

A book is seldom the product of one person's effort alone. I am deeply grateful to Mrs. Martin H. Franzmann for her letters and for the material which she was able to provide; to Peter Franzmann for insights into the Franzmann family at home; and to Martin's brothers, Werner, William, and Gerhardt, and to his sister, Helen Katt, for their family memories. I owe a great debt to Dr. Carl Schalk for his guidance and for the foreward to this book. Thanks also must be given to Barry Bobb of Concordia Publishing House for all the time and effort he put in to making this book a reality. And, finally, I am grateful to my wife, Carolyn, for her patience, support, and careful proofreading.

Richard N. Brinkley

Concordia Publishing House also expresses its thanks to Henry Gerike for his many hours of additional research into theological writings of Dr. Franzmann. We also express our gratitude to the various copyright holders for permission to quote from their works, including: Dr. Gale Eifrig, editor of "The Cresset" for Kenneth Korby's eulogy; Dr. Bruce Backer, author of *Lutheran Worship: A Course Guide*; Lutheran Council in the U.S.A. (LCUSA) for the text "O God, O Lord of Heaven and Earth; Pastor Russell E. Falzman, editor of the *The American Lutheran* for the excerpt from F. R. Webber's article "The Fine Arts in the Service of the Church"; and the Wisconsin Evangelical Lutheran Synod (WELS) for reprint rights to Dr. Franzmann's article "Christian Poetry" from the *Northwestern Lutheran*.

The following hymns written by Dr. Franzmann are now in the public domain:

Christ, Our Lord, Arose

Jesus, Only, Naught But Jesus

O Lord, We Praise Thee

O Thou, Whose Fiery Blessing

Our Lord Has Laid His Benison

Praise Thou the Lord, My Soul

Thou Art the Christ, the Son

The Dawn Has Driven Dark Night Away

To Songs of Joy Awake Thee

The following hymns are under copyright by Concordia Publishing House:

In Adam We Have All Been One

O Fearful Place, Where He Who Knows Our Heart

O Kingly Love, That Faithfully

O Thou, Who Hast of Thy Pure Grace

Rise Again, Ye Lion-Hearted

Thy Strong Word

With High Delight Let Us Unite

Franzmann's translation "Isaiah in a Vision Did of Old" is copyrighted by *Lutheran Book of Worship*. Likewise "Weary of All Trumpeting" is held by the Inter-Lutheran Commission on Worship.

The following are copyrighted by the Franzmann family and used with their permission:

Thy Word Has Been Our Daily Bread

O Thou, Who on Th' Accursed Ground

Preach You the Word

Contents

Foreword

The hymnic legacy of the poet/theologian Martin Hans Franzmann (1907–76)—encompassing a body of both original texts and translations—has left a distinct, unique, and significant imprint on 20th-century American hymnody. Such original hymns as "Thy Strong Word Did Cleave the Darkness," "In Adam We Have All Been One," "Weary of All Trumpeting," "O God, O Lord of Heaven and Earth," and "O Kingly Love That Faithfully," have found their way into many hymnals. And such translations as "With High Delight Let Us Unite" and "Isaiah in a Vision Did of Old" continue to sing their way into the hearts of countless Christian congregations.

Franzmann was one of the first real poets to emerge among Lutherans in the 20th century. Early in his college career examples of his secular verse—in both German and English—appeared in the literary journals of both Northwestern Preparatory School and the College in Thiensville, Wisconsin, where he was a student. Both his classical education (which shaped and honed his literary skills) and the pastoral scenes of Wisconsin (where he grew up and went to school) were obvious sources of influence and inspiration. Titles of such early poems as "To the Mississippi," "Heil'ge Nacht," "Belshazzar," "A Sonnet," "Hellas," or "Apology for Greek Syntax" reflect his background and the breadth of his interests (see Appendix III).

However, it was Arthur Katt, pastor of St. Peter's Lutheran Church in Shaker Heights, Ohio, where Martin and his new wife were teaching, who was, perhaps, most responsible for urging Franzmann to use his literary skills in the cause of hymnody. In 1934—with the publication of *Christian Hymns*, a small collection of six translations and one original hymn prepared for use by the Shaker Heights congregation—Franzmann's early hymnic efforts first saw the light of day. The years that followed saw the writing of additional hymn texts and translations by Franzmann, each usually called forth by some specific occasion or request. At his death in 1976 Franzmann's hymns and translations consisted of an exceptionally significant—even if a relatively small—body of texts.

9

Characterized by a "rough-cast ruggedness," by lines that soar, but most of all by finely-honed texts deeply rooted in a theology of Law and Gospel, sin and salvation, Word and Sacrament, Franzmann's hymns may not always reveal their depth and richness upon the first reading or singing. Upon closer acquaintance, however, their profound magnificence reveals itself in new, surprising, and often unexpected ways. If some texts are seen as too rich, too dense, too theologically packed to be of popular appeal, Franzmann shoots back: "Who says hymns have to be easy?" Erik Routley, commenting on Franzmann's clear Law/Gospel approach, suggests that "his hymns seem always to frown before they smile," and notes that "this in itself is a refreshment after the fixed and euphoric beam that we got from some earlier American poets." Another, speaking of Franzmann's translations, suggests that they are "reminiscent of the high and noble work of [John Mason] Neale and [Robert] Bridges."

Franzmann had little patience with what he called "shoddy Ersatz hymnody." Those who parrot the tired arguments that hymns must be easy to sing, that a passion for perfection is undemocratic snobbery, or who excuse the use of inferior hymns as temporary stepping stones to something better, had best be prepared for Franzmann's sharp words from *Ha! Ha! Among the Trumpets* (soon to be re-released by Concordia).

His use of little-known or less-commonly-used words, his skillful turn of phrase to bring out a new or unsuspected meaning, his use of what today is viewed as antiquated language, all seem to be so out of touch with current politically correct ideas of what the language of 20th-century hymnody should be. Yet we ignore these magnificent texts to our own impoverishment and alter them at the cost of an enfeebled language.

Richard Brinkley carefully leads us into the life and work of this gift of God to the church and describes the circumstances which gave rise to a body of hymn texts which have become well-loved vehicles for the expression of the faith. "Franzmann," Brinkley says, "was a man graced by God with many talents, but at heart he was a poet. It is evident from reading his writings, particularly his sermons and devotional writings, that the song of poetry, God's song, was in his heart." For those who knew Franzmann only through

his hymnody, the sampling of his theological articles and books will be an additional, unexpected delight. This little volume gathers together the fruits of that exceptional talent and makes it available to all.

In the final stanza of his "O God, O Lord of Heaven and Earth"—written for the 450th anniversary of the Reformation, and as the storm clouds of division were beginning to gather over his own church—Franzmann prayed:

O Spirit, who didst once restore
Thy Church that it might be again
The bringer of good news to men,
Breathe on Thy cloven Church once more,
That in these gray and latter days
There may be men whose life is praise,
Each life a high doxology
To Father, Son, and unto Thee.

Those of us who have experienced the glory of his magnificent texts can only believe that the gift to the church of the life and work of this great singer of songs—Martin Franzmann—was God's boundless and inestimable answer to that very prayer.

Carl Schalk
June 1993

1

The Life of Martin Franzmann

A BRIEF BIOGRAPHY AND A SAMPLING OF HIS THEOLOGICAL WRITINGS

Martin Franzmann was born on January 29, 1907 in Lake City, Minnesota, and baptized on February 17 of the same year. His father, William Franzmann, an immigrant from the Westphalia region of Germany, served as the pastor of a dual parish—St. John's Lutheran Church in Lake City and Emmanuel Lutheran Church in West Florence. His mother, Else (also the child of an immigrant) made music, in particular Christian hymns, an important part of the Franzmann's family daily life together.[1] This had a profound influence on the children as two became talented hymnwriters (Werner and Martin).

Martin was such an avid reader that it became a matter of concern to his parents who encouraged him continually to go outside and get some exercise. He learned to play the cello and was familiar enough with the piano to chord accompaniments for the songs he would create around old hymn and folksong melodies. By the time Martin was ready to go off to Northwestern Preparatory School, he was known for his incredibly facile mind [2] This attribute proved a great gift which he would later employ to full advantage as a theologian and hymnwriter.

While at prep school, he quickly distinguished himself as a poet. He composed a number of poems for the school's literary journal, *Black and Red*. (Some of these appear in Appendix III.) His facility with words would show itself in various ways. While engaged in setting up the school auditorium for some event, Martin would make up a song with a story line that included everyone present and would spontaneously put this to a little melody with a

13

refrain that everyone could join in singing! When home from school, he would entertain his brothers by conjuring up an intricate story and challenging them to catch him in some inconsistency or contradiction. Franzmann seemed to have an almost limitless vocabulary. This command of language is reflected in all his writing: poems, prayers, hymns, translations, commentaries, sermons, and theological discourses. He had the ability to reach a person at what one of his students referred to as a "visceral" level, more than just the mind, but the touching the innermost recesses of the person.[3]

The Board of Control of Northwestern College thought so highly of him, that upon graduation he was offered a position as an instructor in Greek and English. He served there two years before going on to Wisconsin Lutheran Seminary in 1930. This being the days of the Great Depression, his education was interrupted a number of times. Most significant was the time he spent teaching at St. Peter's Lutheran School in Shaker Heights, Ohio (1933–1935). It was here that Martin became acquainted with Pastor Arthur Katt, a man with a deep interest in hymnology. Pastor Katt immediately recognized Martin's talent with languages and encouraged him to make a series of hymn translations.[4] The result of his first effort was a series of six hymn translations and one original hymn. St. Peter's published these in a small booklet entitled *Christian Hymns* in 1934.

Following his teaching tenure in Shaker Heights, Franzmann re-enrolled at the Seminary and graduated in 1936. Following his graduation, he was again offered a position as Professor of Classics at Northwestern College. In 1946 he received a call to teach New Testament Exegetical Theology at Concordia Seminary, St. Louis, Missouri.

Franzmann took up his position as Professor of New Testament Interpretation under the encouragement and leadership of Dr. William Arndt, chairman of the Department of Exegetical Theology. It was during those years at Concordia Theological Seminary that Franzmann began his career as a writer in earnest. He was now drawn into the full course of the church's activities, serving many times as essayist and/or participant at conferences, conventions, and as a member of various boards and commissions. It was also during those years that the major part of his hymnwriting was done. His first article, published after joining the Seminary faculty, was "So We

Preach" in the April 1947 edition of the *Lutheran Witness*. A reflection on the centennial of The Lutheran Church—Missouri Synod, it gives focus to the central purpose of the church, that is, to preach the gospel of Jesus Christ. An example of the proclamation of Law and Gospel, the article is as much forward looking as it reflects the past and the present. Noteworthy are the comments about the kind of church the Lutheran church is, especially since the LCMS was emerging as an English-speaking church, departing from its German language heritage. The words give today's church pause for reflection—

> "The power of God unto salvation to everyone that believeth; to the Jew first, and also the Greek"—that is the Gospel. And the whole meaning and the whole glory of our hundred years' history lies solely in the fact that we have preached that Gospel without additions, without abridgment, and without reservations. What we have offered the world is simply God's offer of salvation, implemented and guaranteed by God's power. . . .

> We offer, not something of our own, not a system to be followed, not a set of rules to be obeyed, not a wisdom to be assayed and absorbed; we offer a power, the power of God that delivers. . . .

> And we offer this salvation to all mankind, to everyone that believeth, to all the world; that is to say, to all the guilty, for God's grace extends as far as His judgment. That is what we have been doing these hundred years, that is what we are doing now, we "exclusive" Lutherans that will not dip our feet into the stream of a unionistic ecumenicity, we narrowhearted Lutherans, we dogmatical hairsplitters, we that have bound ourselves hand and foot —yea, brain, will, desire, heart, soul, and all—to a Book that will not let us go. We offer salvation to all. We offer it more freely because we know it more truly.

> We lay down no conditions. We ask none to take any man's word as authority over him or any man's power to dominate him. It is God's Word that we ask men to succumb to. There are no conditions; only believe. We demand no performance. We ask no one to climb laborious ladders to a probable heaven. We ask men to believe and to let God work. We place no bars—racial, political, or social. The Lutheran Church is not a German church, an English church, or a Chinese church; it is neither a white man's

church nor a black man's church; neither a rich man's church nor a poor man's church. The Gospel that we preach is a universal Gospel and the grace it offers is universal grace.

So we preach. We cannot do otherwise; our life principle is the Spirit of God; and if we live by the Spirit, we must also walk by the Spirit. In so preaching, whatever our shortcomings may have been, lies the glory of our past. In so preaching lies the only hope of our future. There is no conflict between conserving and going forward; for unless we conserve this, our life, we shall not go forward at all.

"Return to 'Primacy of Exegesis'" appeared in the June 1947 edition of *Concordia Theological Monthly*.[5] It was a review of the first issue of *Interpretation, A Journal of Bible and Theology*. Franzmann concedes that there are elements of "critical study" throughout the journal, but notes "a serious theological concern with the Bible. . . as the inscripturation of God's revelation of Himself, a thorough-going renunciation of the vicious, condescending attitude toward the Word which has blighted Scriptural studies these many years." The journal is recommended by Franzmann "as an aid and stimulus" to Lutheran theologians and students with the caution that "the journal is not a Lutheran journal; but it speaks a language that is at least a dialect of the ecumenical Lutheran language and contains much that warms the Lutheran heart."

In 1948 the Lutheran churches of Germany, Finland, Norway, Holland, and the United States met at the small, South German resort town of Bad Boll, Wurttemberg, nestled at the foot of the Swabian Alps. This was the first of a series of conferences held throughout Europe that were commonly known as either the Bad Boll Conferences or the Lutheran Free Conferences. At these conferences the various Lutheran churches shared and discussed their understandings of Scripture and the Lutheran Confessions.

The 1949 conferences had as their major theme "The Way of Salvation According to Scripture and the Lutheran Confessions" and were divided up into four sessions. The third and fourth sessions focused on "Lutheran Dogma According to Scripture and the Confessions." It was here that Franzmann presented his paper entitled "Augustana II: Of Original Sin," which was later published in the December 1949 edition of *Concordia Theological Monthly*. This arti-

cle illustrates well Franzmann's art of exegesis in the service of systematic theology. Throughout the article he shows how "repeatedly, and blow upon blow, the hammer of the Word of God is made to fall on any self-assertion of man before his God, on every claim to righteousness which man, as man, dares make. Nothing is left to the pride and conceit of man. The whole man is a sinner, conceived and born in sin . . . incapable of true fear of God, incapable of trust in God. . . .What must happen, if man is to find a gracious God, is not mere alteration or improvement, but complete renovation, a creative act of God." The article, an excellent proclamation of Law and Gospel, concludes—

> This alienation from God, this enmity towards Him, is not in the first instance an act, but is the whole bent of man, the whole set of his heart, the *perpetua naturae inclinatio* of which the Apology speaks. This *perpetua inclinatio* is then actualized in evil deeds: "For **from within**, out of the heart of men, proceed evil thoughts, adulteries, fornications, murders . . . " (Mark 7:21) . . . In St. John, too, the sinful impulse and the sinful act take place in an atmosphere that is already sin: "He that hateth his brother **is in darkness and walketh in darkness** and knoweth not whither he goeth, because that darkness **hath blinded** his eyes" (1 John 2:11). Sin here is a controlling reality that leads men inevitably to sinning. It is hardly necessary to pursue the proof further; the proof is everywhere, not only where sin is specifically dealt with, but also in such concepts as "rebirth" and "Repentance" (*metanoia*), which presuppose a complete break with the old man, a total reversal of all that man naturally is—the follower of Jesus must deny **himself**. (Mark 8:34).
>
> Our Confessions speak of the doctrine of original sin as a "necessary article." It remains such, a necessary article, today and for today's preaching. The antithesis—man before God, and man in his striving for self-assertion and self-sufficiency—has grown no less acute since the sixteenth century; and the theology of the nineteenth century has left in its wake a blunted consciousness of sin that makes the preachment of sin in all its Biblical force necessary as never before. Moreover, grace and sin, faith and repentance, cannot be sundered.

Franzmann would serve as a delegate and presenter at three Bad Boll Conferences. In 1953 his paper was on "Jesus the Con-

sumator"[6] and was published in the *Concordia Theological Monthly* under the title, "Christ, the Hope of Glory" in the December 1953 edition. Based on 2 Timothy 4:18, this article was an exegetical paper on the "characteristics of the eschatological hope of the Church of Jesus Christ. For that hope is (1) a Christ-centered hope; it is (2) a hope that looks for a divine act of deliverance; it is (3) a hope for a **total** consummation; it is (4) a "practical" hope; and (5) it is doxological." From the final section—

> The doxology in 2 Tim. 4:18 refers to Christ, to be sure, but Christ has His full glory when God the Father is glorified. At His birth angels sang glory to God in the highest, and His ministry from beginning to end sought the glory of the Father, who sent Him (John 8:50; 7:18; . . .). When Satan tempts Him to use His divine Sonship for obtaining independent glory, He meets that temptation with a triumphant "It is written" that thrice affirms the sole glory of the only God (Matt. 4:4, 7, 10). When He called men to repentance, He called upon them to turn from the self-assertion and self-insistence of their sin, their wild and rebellious dreams of self-glory, and to take seriously in mind, heart, will, and deed the glory of the reign of God that was come to them in His Person. He will not seek or accept fame as a worker of wonders; He commands silence when His wondrous deed is done, for He is the quietly working servant of Jahweh, who will not strive nor cry aloud (Matt. 12:16f). . . . On the eve of His Passion, Jesus prays: "Father, glorify Thy name" (John 12:28), and here, too, he sees His own glory in His Father's glorification (John 17:16). When He goes to the cross, He is "savoring" the things of God (Matt. 16:23); He humbles Himself and becomes obedient unto death in order that at the end of all, when God by His glory has raised Him from the dead (Rom. 6:4) and has highly exalted Him and given Him the name above every name and all the universe bows before Him and acclaims Him Lord, it may all be "to the glory of God, the Father" (Phil. 2:6ff).

The 1956 sessions were held in London, Uelzen, Berlin, and Oberursel. Franzmann's presentation for this series of conferences was entitled "The Apostolate: Its Enduring Significance in the Apostolic Word" and was published in the March 1957 edition of the *Concordia Theological Monthly.* Using the Lutheran Confessions (*Of the Summary Content, Rule,* and *Standard, Formula of Concord,*

Epitome 1) as a starting point, Franzmann again uses his skill as an exegete in supporting systematic theology—

The conception "apostle" and "apostolic" is one which is determined entirely by its relationship to the Lord, who establishes the apostolate and sends the apostles. . . .

The New Testament apostle is determined wholly by the Lord Jesus; he is therefore a creation of God's grace, and this grace is, first of all, pure giving. The gift character of this grace is marked in Matthew 16 by the fact that the initiative in the disciples' confession of Jesus as the Christ lies completely with Jesus. . . . It is Jesus who provokes the confession; it is Jesus who points out its significance; and it is Jesus who gives the apostle Peter his function and his authority.

The disciples do not select their rabbi; Jesus **calls** His disciples, and they obey His call as the Messianic call that it is. Over their discipleship is written the word of Jesus: "Ye have not chosen Me, but I have chosen you" (John 15:16). . . .

The apostolic Word, written or re-echoed in the living voice of "apostolic" men created by the apostolic Word, is the enduring embodiment of Jesus' "Lo, I am with you alway, even unto the end of the world". . . .

In the apostolic Word the church perpetually hears the voice of the Good Shepherd, with its note of graciously free bestowal, "The kingdom of heaven is at hand," and, at the same time, with its note of gracious and inexorable demand, "Repent." . . .

The grace of God at work in the apostolic Word calls for a church which knows that it exists and lives by God's giving . . . which knows that it can live only by giving what it has received, giving as freely as it has received . . . .

The apostolic Word calls for a church which wills to live of the Word of its Lord; which in repentance lets that Word judge and renew her and thus finds the strength for renunciation, self-denial, and the cross; a church for which "success," wholly or in part, is not a determining factor; a church which puts obedience first and lets success come *ubi et quando visum est Deo* . . . ["where and when it pleases God," Augsburg Confession, Article 5].

Who stands in the apostolic succession? The answer cannot be divorced from the apostolic Word. The apostles in their Word

are intent upon creating men in their own image: "Be ye followers of me, even as I also am of Christ" (1 Cor. 11:1 . . .). The church which gives ear to the apostolic Word and gives its heart to the Lord, who in that apostolic Word calls for the heart; the church which becomes "apostolic" in obedient mimesis [imitation] under that Word; the church which awaits the coming of the Lord in joyously energetic hope and in holy fear—that church stands in the apostolic succession in a sense and in a reality which no unbrokenly successive imposition of palms on pates can guarantee.

"Theological Conferences in Europe—Summer 1956" was primarily a report to The Lutheran Church—Missouri Synod concerning these talks. Far from making the conferences seem routine and mundane, Franzmann gives flesh and bone to the intangible talks in far away Europe by giving personal insight and reflection. Because he did little writing specifically on worship and hymnody, noteworthy are his comments in this article—

> The church has a right to ask about results [of this conference]; and the church likewise has the wisdom to know that 'results' are not always of a kind that can be completely known, fully evaluated, and crisply entered in a ledger. Still, we have not only our own feelings, but the sincere and unsought words of our brethren to assure us of the fact that the Lord of the Church has of His grace used us to serve our brethren, that we have been instrumental, for example, in bringing the various branches of the German free churches closer together, that we have opened and helped to carry on discussions which have served to clarify and to consolidate their theological thinking and willing—and the fact that these discussions opened up new questions which invite further common work should be viewed as a gift also; for theology is like the Christ life, as Luther once described it, not a "having become" but a "becoming." The ever-renewed report of what God has wrought among us in America, without our merit and despite our faults, in the way of a live and dynamic congregational life, in witness and stewardship, is having its effect on the congregational life of our brethren abroad. . . .

> But in the life of the church, results are always a mutual matter; he who brings gifts also receives gifts. At least one member of this year's group can report that he has come back with a

whole roster of experiences and impressions which will make his ministry in the church a better one. . . . glimpses given us into the life of the territorial churches in Germany, for instance, the difficulties and agonies of men who seek to maintain a really and rigorously Lutheran confessional position in a system which all but demands something less of a man; the measured and unhurried solemnity of the Sunday service of the Free Church congregation at Grosz-Oesingen, where the Blaschor trumpets chorales in the churchyard for half an hour before the service for all to hear, where a two-hour service is not considered a penitential exercise, where the whole congregation moves through the massive melody of hymn and chant with an assurance which only a long tradition can give; Sunday service in Berlin at the church . . . where the pastor and two members of his vestry kneel before a small altar in the sacristy in mutual intercession before the service begins, a beautiful and telling exemplification of the relationship between the ministry and the royal priesthood of all believers; where communicants step before the altar to hear the confessional address and kneel at the altar for individual absolution (a last remnant of the old Lutheran private confession). . . .

And much more besides: the circle of one's intercessions is enlarged by such a mission and such contacts; and this report can hardly close on a better note than an appeal to all the church to remember in prayer our brethren in England, Germany, and France, men striving in weakness like ours to serve the Lord, who is our Lord, struggling with difficulties greater than ours, with means less than ours.

The year 1950 was a significant year because Franzmann was appointed to two important committees on which he would serve for many years to come. The first was the Committee on English Bible Translations. He served on this committee until 1956, and in 1962, he wrote an article "Why So Many Bibles" for the *Lutheran Witness* in which he defended the new translations of the Bible as being necessary for four reasons. First, the English language is constantly changing, and periodic updates of the language in translation are useful. Second, scholarship has improved our understanding of the languages of the Bible with the result that we can make more accurate translations of many biblical passages. Third, we have a better understanding, from an historical point of view, of the New Testament times, which enables us to translate more accurately the

way in which the Scriptures would have been understood by the people of that time. And finally, we have better, older texts of the scriptures, texts that were not available to previous generations of translators. The result is we have more accurate understandings of the texts themselves and the times in which they were written.[7]

Another important committee to which Franzmann was appointed in 1950 was the Synodical Committee on Doctrinal Unity, commonly called the Doctrinal Unity Committee. The 1935 convention of the Missouri Synod at Cleveland, Ohio, created this committee as the result of overtures from the American Lutheran Church and the United Lutheran Church. These two church bodies wished to establish closer relations with the Missouri Synod and, eventually, to achieve pulpit and altar fellowship. The committee originally was known as the Committee on Lutheran Church Union and consisted of five men appointed by the convention. The committee eventually grew to eight and then 10 members. The 1953 convention of the LCMS gave the committee the status of a standing committee of the Synod, and in 1962, it became known as the Commission on Theology and Church Relations or simply the CTCR. Franzmann served as vice chairman of this committee from 1950 until he left the Seminary in 1969. Service on the CTCR placed Franzmann in the midst of a number of controversial matters, not the least of which was the crumbling of the Synodical Conference over questions of externals, prayer, fellowship with other Lutheran church bodies, and the advisability of calling for a free conference of all Lutherans. The request for this free conference had been an action taken by Dr. J.W. Behnken at the request of the College of Presidents of the LCMS on May 6, 1949.[8]

In 1952 Franzmann was also appointed to the Synodical Conference where he served in the capacity of secretary. These were troubled times in the Synodical Conference, which was made up of four conservative Lutheran Synods: the Missouri Synod, the Wisconsin Synod, the Slovak Synod, and the Norwegian Synod. It was an especially difficult time for Franzmann himself since two of his brothers, Werner and Gerhard, served in the Wisconsin Synod. This was the Synod in which Franzmann had been raised, and through whose schools he had received the majority of his education. Franzmann left this committee in 1956. The situation continued to degen-

erate to the point where the Synodical Conference was finally disbanded in 1961 and the various synods which made up the Conference began to go their separate ways.[9]

It would appear that Franzmann was a man of great energy who would not say "no" when asked to serve the church. The meeting of the Lutheran World Federation was held in Hanover, Germany, in the summer of 1952, and Martin was there as an official representative of The Lutheran Church—Missouri Synod. His attendance at this meeting arose out of his membership on the Doctrinal Unity Committee which was given the task of making official contacts with the Lutheran World Federation.[10]

In the summer of 1954 Franzmann was at the Institute of the Lutheran Association for Human Relations held at Valparaiso University. Here he presented a paper entitled "The Christian Hope and Our Fellow Man," which was published in the October 1955 edition of *Concordia Theological Monthly*. It is primarily an exegetical paper on James. The application of the Gospel is still relevant today—

> What are we? We are God's children by a new redemptive birth. Where are we? We are His people in an alien world, a world still in rebellion against Him, still in the power of the Evil One (1 John 5:19). God's great act of liberation is at the same time His act of laying claim upon us. Therefore James 1:18, the great indicative of redemption, is followed by 1:19, the great imperative: "Know it, my beloved brethren." To **know** God (and we know Him by what He does) is to acknowledge Him as God, to let Him be God in everything; to know Him in hope is to assert here and now the new world where God is all and all. Our feckless and misdirected lives come under the Lordship of the Lord Jesus Christ, the Lord of Glory, and from Him receive purpose and direction, so that knowing means **hearing**, and hearing means doing, and doing is worship—the God we know is the God who has acted for us, is acting, and will act; to worship Him in Spirit and in truth is to worship Him in act (1:26, 27).
>
> Hope, committal to God's new world, involves us here and now, commits us here and now, to God's view of the poor and outcast, the honorless and the submerged, compels us to see men with God's eyes and to deal with men, all men, with God's mercy. It is no accident that James 2:1–13, the section which deals with "respect of person's" rings with the great keywords of the Christ-

23

ian proclamation—James is pointing us to where we are and to what we are: election, inheritance, kingdom of God, promise, mercy, and Judgment. Yes, Judgment; for the God who justifies remains, for James as for Paul, God the Judge. Only mercy, God's mercy, will save us at that Judgment; but whether or not we have committed ourselves to that mercy will be seen concretely in the fact that we have or have not been merciful to our brother man; whether our hope in, and our confession to, that mercy has been dominated and active in our whole life.

Two things occurred in 1956 which had a significant impact on Franzmann's career. The first was the Springfield Seminary awarding him the honorary degree of Doctor of Divinity "for his outstanding academic contributions and achievements as well as for his service and dedication to Lutheranism and the work of the Christian Church."[11] Franzmann had been working on an advanced degree since the early 1930s when he had been a student at the University of Chicago. He had also attended the University of Chicago in the late 1940s and early 1950s working on his PhD: "Legal Image and Legal Language in Greek Tragedy"—a degree which he never completed.[12]

The second important event was his selection as head of the Department of Exegetical Theology to replace Dr. Arndt who had retired. It must be kept in mind, throughout the 10 years from 1946 through 1956, that Franzmann, in addition to all the committees, conferences, essays, and periodical contributions (over 30 articles), was a full-time member of the Seminary faculty taking on his share of the teaching load.

The Doctrinal Unity Committee sponsored an International Conference of Theologians in June 1959. This conference was held at Concordia Lutheran College, Oakland, California on the topic of "Our Fellowship under Scripture." Franzmann attended this meeting and presented a paper titled "The Posture of the Interpreter," which later appeared in the January 1960 edition of the *Concordia Theological Monthly*. This article rings true yet today, especially for pastors, teachers, theologians, and seminarians. The conclusion—

> What, then, is the posture of the interpreter? It is the posture of the obedient hearer and the overawed beholder. He hears the verdict of the righteous God of the Law without evasion or attempts at self-defense; he hears with all defenses down. He

looks upon the God of grace as He reveals Himself in the face of His Son and says with Job: "Now mine eye seeth Thee; wherefore I abhor myself and repent in dust and ashes" (Job 42: 5–6).

If he abhors himself, he is set free for God, and his posture is the posture of adoration. His task of interpretation is a priestly ministration of the Word. He sees in the apostolate the vehicle by which God's last Word comes to him, the token and evidence of God's infinite condescension, a manifesting of God's impetus toward incarnation, and he glorifies the God who has given such authority to men.

His heart burns within him as he hears the Word, and he hastens to tell his brethren. The vision that overawes him also sets him to work; like Paul, he is not disobedient to the heavenly vision. His posture is the posture of ministry.

The initial chapter of Franzmann's first book, *The Word of the Lord Grows*, appeared in the *Concordia Theological Monthly* in August 1959. This book, which was eventually published by Concordia Publishing House in 1961 (and is still in print), was an attempt by Franzmann to provide an introduction to the world of the New Testament, which he felt was lacking for students and laypeople studying that part of the Scriptures.

In the late summer of 1960 Franzmann was at the Counselors and Fiscal Conference held at Valparaiso University. Much of the conference was devoted to a discussion of doctrinal issues. Franzmann presented a paper on "Revelation—Scripture—Interpretation." In it he defended the inerrancy of Scripture and criticized the "historico-critical" method's "demythologization," which he felt "cuts the heart out of the New Testament message."[13]

The Lutheran Church of Australia has had many contacts with The Lutheran Church—Missouri Synod over the years. One of these was as part of the Convention of the Australian Lutheran Church at Melbourne in 1962. Franzmann attended this convention as an official representative of the St. Louis Seminary and made a presentation to the convention.[14]

Another series of conferences attended by Franzmann were in South America in January 1965. The first was at Porto Allegre at the theological conference of the Brazil District and then on to Buenos Aires to a conference with leaders of the Argentine Lutheran

Church. At these meetings Franzmann presented a paper titled "Hermeneutical Dilemma: Dualism in the Interpretation of Holy Scripture." Later he presented the same paper to the St. Louis Pastors' Conference of the LCMS. The text of the paper was published in the *Concordia Theological Monthly* in September 1965. Franzmann uses Kurt Frör's *Biblische Hermeneutik* as a foil for an outline of the dilemma dealing with the question of history and interpretation: the historical method and dualism in Biblical interpretation. Note especially the allusion to the liturgy—

> Exegesis [is] a ministry whose task is to let the Christ grow great before the church's eyes.
>
> With this prophetic conception of history we are in a position to see the secularized conception of history for what it is, how it differs at every point from history as conceived of and written by prophets and apostles, the spokesmen of the Lord of the future in purposeful conversation with His people. Here **God** is in the center and is all in all; there, fallen **man** in the *mataiotes* [futile thinking] (Rom. 1:21) of his mind. Here the Word is **the** power in history; there the Word is distrusted—the father of the lie has made it serve the **lie**. . . . Here the **future** is always being opened up by the Word of God; there the future is a closed door, a blank wall.
>
> Frustrated man in his frustrated world **must** make legends; he must gild the facts of his existence, or he cannot endure them. He has no future, and so he has need for dreams. Frustrated man **must**, in virtue of his godless *mataiotes*, reinterpret and vary. But the prophets and apostles and the apostolic church, who worship the LORD who changes not and serve the Lord Jesus Christ who is the same yesterday, today, and forever, **they** have no need for variation. Theirs is the inexhaustible Word of the constant God, unchanging amid all the changes of history, inexhaustibly rich for every need of man in a changing world. The Christian interpreter is set free not **for** variation but **from** the need and compulsion to vary. Finally, the Promise and the Gospel of God is God's No! to that history of alienated man which ends monotonously with "And he died." To measure the probabilities of the creative action of God's Word in history by the "laws" of that history is as fruitless as it is perverse. . . .

26

In emphasizing what needs emphasizing, the miracle of the Bible . . . we run the risk of ignoring its historical character, with all the splendid color and variety that belongs to history. . . .

How shall we escape that danger? The only sure way and safe way is to observe the inspired texts themselves, to be wholly and completely open to the operation of the Spirit who originated them and does His work through them. . . .

The Spirit's sovereign freedom in confiscating any and every facet of human experience and history for His purposes **can** be (and has been) misinterpreted as a servile borrowing; thus the Scriptures come to be viewed as a product of their environment, as one more product of the human spirit and not **the** product of **the** Spirit. . . .

We need to remember that the historical work is only the stairway leading to the door of the text; when we have climbed it, we can see **what** door and **what kind of** door we stand before and desire to enter. (That is, we recognize the text in its particularity and its uniqueness.) It is not the key that unlocks the door, to be sure; the door is unlocked from within. But it would be both senseless and a mark of ingratitude toward the God who builds stairways to despise the stairway just because it is not the key. . . .

[Another danger occurs] when we see how the historical method dissolves the records of the mighty acts of God into myth and legend, [that] we are inclined to react in the opposite direction. We incline toward making of the true and indispensable principle of the *sensus literalis* [literal sense] a dry schematism, a pattern that we impose on the texts rather than find in the text. The God who created birds and inspired the psalms is a poet, the Poet; that is a fact we dare not forget. . . .

The prophetic-interpretive representation of an event employing symbols does not call into question the historicity of the event. . . .To recognize the presence and value of symbolic language in a narrative where it is probable and recognizable is one thing; it is quite another thing to make of the reality corresponding to the symbol a mere symbol. . . .

There is a danger here; if we recognize it, we are forewarned against it and can avoid it. If we in panic fear refuse to face this characteristic of the inspired texts, we are ignoring what the Psalter and the whole history of Christian hymnody has taught

us: That the language of poetry is the most powerful, the most moving, and in the last analysis, the truest and most accurate form of speech. . . .

A word should be said regarding the hermeneutical function of the liturgy, that other great gift of God to the Lutheran Church. The Lutheran liturgy provides an ideal setting for this "decisive interpretation of Scripture." Here the movement of the church year is a constant reminder of the eschatological character of our interpretation of Scripture, for here we are continually reminded that God is "on the way," in movement toward His last goal of judgment and consummation—and we are reminded, too, that we the church are the wandering people of God, on the way, looking toward the city that has foundations. Here the eschatological horizon is perpetually being opened up, in the confession of sins and in absolution, in the praise, prayer, proclamation, and confession of faith, in the receiving of the blessing of God, for "I will bless thee" is both the primeval and the eschatological Word of God to His people (Gen. 12:2; Matt. 25:34).

And here in the liturgy, Word and Sacrament are kept together in their essential and organic unity. This unity of Word and Sacrament is a perpetual reminder to the proclaiming interpreter that he is not in the last analysis "dealing with" the Word of God; he is being dealt with by the God who in His Word is present and active to judge and to save. Here, too, the eschatological horizon is opened up, when we are taught to conceive of the Word of God thus, we know that every proclamation of it is an anticipation of the Last Judgment. For with every proclamation the Light goes forth into the world: "And this is the judgment, that the light has come into the world, and men loved darkness rather than light, because their deeds were evil . . . but he who does what is true comes to the light, that it may be clearly seen that his deeds have been wrought in God. (John 3:19, 21)

From 1960 onward Franzmann worked more on larger writing tasks and less on essays and articles for periodicals. In the same year as *The Word of the Lord Grows* appeared (1961), *Follow Me* was published by Concordia. This was a study on the gospel of Matthew in which Franzmann, much like Bonhoeffer before him, explored the cost involved in being a disciple of Christ Jesus. In 1963 *New Courage for Daily Living*, a series of devotions, was published. Two books were completed in 1966: *Ha! Ha! Among the Trumpets*, which

was a collection of sermons (soon to be re-released by Concordia), and *Grace Under Pressure,* a book co-authored with F. Dean Lueking. *Concordia Commentary: Romans* is, as its title suggests, a commentary on Paul's letter to the Romans, and was published in 1968 (and is still available). In this period only nine articles by Franzmann appeared in the church's periodicals.

As a teacher Franzmann was highly regarded by his students. First of all, they were impressed by his knowledge of the Greek New Testament. He knew large portions of it by heart and could recite to them from memory without having to consult a Greek New Testament. He also had a way with words born of his love for languages and for the English language in particular. Franzmann would conduct his classes by reading rapidly from his prepared notes. Many students found it difficult to take notes and many stopped taking notes in class. Rather they would listen intently and then return to their rooms to reconstruct what they had absorbed from the lecture.[15] He demanded much of his students but gave them much also. One of his former students wrote, in regard to his teaching:

> I incline to regard St. Martin's advice to us seminary students a kind of oxymoronic aphorism: "To understand the New Testament," he said, "read the Old Testament." Those words were not just advice to students; they reflected his own practice.[16]

In 1968 Franzmann took a sabbatical in which he traveled to Salzburg, Austria, and then on to Newton Farrers in England, where he spent about six months.

While in England, Franzmann became reacquainted with the Evangelical Lutheran Church of England and with its seminary, Westfield House at Cambridge, where his son John was studying for the ministry. A lifelong Anglophile, he made the decision in 1969 to leave the St. Louis Seminary and move to Cambridge, England.

As he had done while at the St. Louis Seminary, he continued to write for periodicals, present essays, and work on larger writing projects. *Pray for Joy*, a collection of prayers in poetic form, was published in 1970, and, in 1971, the *Concordia Bible with Notes*, which he helped edit, appeared.

By the fall of 1971 it was becoming more and more difficult for Franzmann to keep up with his duties as Tutor. His son, John, began helping him with his work, and, finally, at the beginning of

1972, Martin decided he must resign and allow his son to assume the duties of Tutor at Westfield House.

Franzmann retired to his writing at Wells in Somerset, in the Southwest of England. There he went to work on another devotional book entitled *Alive in the Spirit* which was published by Concordia Publishing House in 1973, and on a study of the Book of Revelation titled *The Revelation of St. John* which came out in 1976. Several hymns can also be attributed to this period of time: "Weary of All Trumpeting" (1972), "Thy Word Has Been Our Daily Bread" (1972), and "O Thou, Who On Th' Accursed Ground" (1974).

Franzmann did return to the United States from time to time. In 1973 he was at the Springfield Seminary where he taught a course entitled "The Art of Exegesis," and where he delivered a chapel sermon on May 22. The text of that sermon was printed in the September 1973 edition of the *Springfielder* with the title "Who Is a God like Thee." It demonstrates the pastoral heart of the preacher—

> Our God forgives; and in His forgiving we have to do, not with a principle, an idea, a conception, but with an **act**. Forgiveness is as actual as the Exodus, as actual as Jacob, as Abraham, as the fathers, as the oath sworn by the living God by His living self—as actual as Jesus of Nazareth, as actual as history under a Roman procurator, *sub Pontio Pilato*, as actual as crucifixion and **resurrection**, "publically portrayed," officially proclaimed by God Himself (Gal. 3:1). Forgiveness is an overt, irreversible act. You may refuse it, but you cannot undo it. You cannot fiddle with it, modify, or remake it. It is **there**, as real as "rise up and walk"— as real as Jesus' "I will; be thou clean."

> This is old stuff; as old as sin itself, almost as old as the hills and the enduring foundations of the earth which the Lord summoned as witnesses against His people (Micah 6:1–5). And, God forgive us, we tend to grow weary of this manna: "our souls loathe this worthless food." We have developed a diseased passion for the "new and improved" theologies. We are told that modern man is no longer in search of a gracious God; he is not looking for forgiveness. His disease is not guilt, but a sense of lostness, insignificance, futility. He feels, not unforgiven but unwanted.

> Conceding for the moment that there is such a thing as "modern man," the question is, obviously, not whether he wants for-

giveness but whether he **needs** it. Does he need it? He seems to have all the symptoms of the unforgiven man. . . .

So, what else is new? Without forgiveness, nothing. "Nothing is strong, nothing is holy." And nothing we can do will make it strong and holy and new. No burnt offerings, no calves a year old, no rivers of oil—no committees, commissions, task forces, cadres, structures, statistics, computers, or all the dreary etcetera of our business. Shall we give our firstborn for our transgressions and the fruit of our body for the sin of our soul? Millions of young men dead in thousands of wars cry out: No! No newness there: and in our day God's trumpets blast that No into every ear. Whatever **we** do, we remain crooked men walking crooked miles and end up being hell to one another in a crooked house. But with forgiveness, then we begin to walk humbly with our God and learn to walk a straight mile, doing justice and loving mercy. Then we can cast our anxieties (which twist us crooked) on Him, the Forgiver, who cares about, who has given His Son for us. Our crooked, constricted hearts are enlarged, and the joy in heaven over one sinner who repents calls forth a new song on earth.

In the spring of 1975 Franzmann returned to the Seminary in St. Louis in order to assist in an attempt to heal the division within the Missouri Synod which followed the walkout of St. Louis Seminary professors and students in 1974. Peter (Franzmann's son) and his wife offered their home as a safe haven for him so he could get some rest, but Franzmann chose to remain on the Seminary campus in a dorm room. As a result he was constantly approached by people who wished to gain his ear on the matter of the synodical division. Franzmann also found himself in the uncomfortable position of middleman between two warring factions. As a result he left St. Louis a tired and dejected man. Those who saw him at this time noted his worn appearance.[17]

In the winter of 1975–76 Franzmann's health began to deteriorate. On Sunday morning, March 28, 1976, Martin Franzmann died peacefully at his apartment in Cambridge at about the same time as the Introit for Laetare was being read— "Rejoice ye with Jerusalem and be glad with her, all ye that love her. Rejoice for joy with her, all ye that mourn for her. Let us go into the house of the Lord."

Franzmann's death was attributed to exhaustion, exhaustion brought on by a spirit that would not, could not, rest from the labors of his ministry.

Kenneth F. Korby, then the editor of *The Cresset*, the literary magazine of Valparaiso University, and a former student of Franzmann, wrote of him in the November/December 1976 edition—

> And then there was Martin H. Franzmann, sweet singer of The Lutheran Church—Missouri Synod. Learned, diligent, hard working, poetic, and a courteous gentleman, Franzmann too was a pilgrim. He was a pilgrim who used the facilities of his travels for shaping the fullness of life that climaxes in being home. The Franzmann home was parabolic of that home which is, and yet is not, here. He relished the sights and sounds and smells of the world and his work. He seemed to me to move by a melody that did not here have a permanent rest. It was a melody clear in its singularity, rich in its polyphony, and sturdy as deep heaven itself. . . .
>
> . . . Franzmann used language the way our university organist, Philip Gehring, uses the Fred and Ella Reddel Memorial Organ in the Chapel of the Resurrection. Franzmann's language could be sparse but evocative as Johann Bengel's, as rich and ornate as Carlyle's, and it could sting like the King's arrows in the heart of the King's enemies. How he popped our ears early in that course: "The Cross is forever the stumbling-block to sentimentality." It is too rare in professorial lectures that learning and truth are combined with a language that is rich and fat, like a great harvest, or delightful and hilarious like a burst of joy. Franzmann often achieved that union; yet, it seemed that he accomplished that union best in his prayers and hymns.[18]

Martin Franzmann died then in the faith of which he so eloquently spoke, wrote, and sang. It may be, when his theological writings are long forgotten on the library shelves, that it will be his hymns which will speak to the hearts of people, and through them the trumpet of God will again sound forth,

> the trumpet none could silence or mistake,
> And blow once more for us and all the world to hear,
>   Living and clear:
>   The feast is ready—come to the feast,
>   The good and the bad,

Come and be glad,
Greatest and least,
Come to the feast![19]

Notes

1 Werner and William Franzmann, interview, May 1992.

2 *Ibid.*

3 Walter Schindler, interview, June 1992.

4 Helen Franzmann Katt, interview, July 1992.

5 Victor A. Bartling, "A Martin Franzmann Bibliography," *Concordia Theological Monthly* 43:6 (June 1972): 485–87.

6 Paul Koenig, "Free Conferences in Europe," *Lutheran Witness* 72 (September 15, 1953): 319–20.

7 Martin H. Franzmann, "Why So Many Bibles?" *Lutheran Witness* 81 (March 20, 1962): 134ff.

8 Alfred O. Fuerbringer and Martin H. Franzmann, "A Quarter Century of Interchurch Relations: 1935–1960," *Concordia Theological Monthly* 32, no. 1 (January 1961): 5–14.

9 Alfred O. Fuerbringer and Martin H. Franzmann, "Reports on Interchurch Relations," *Concordia Theological Monthly* 33, no. 1 (January 1962): 5–12.

10 Alfred O. Fuerbringer and Martin H. Franzmann, *loc. cit.*, pp. 5–14.

11 Bulletin, "The Installation Service of Dr. Martin H. Franzmann, D. D. as Theological Tutor of Westfield House," Westfield House, Cambridge, England, October 4, 1969.

12 Alice Bentzin Franzmann, correspondence, January 1992.

13 Friedrich, E. J., "They Studied Christian Doctrine," *Lutheran Witness* 79: 538–39.

14 John B. Koch, *When the Murray Meets the Mississippi* (North Adelaide, South Australia: Lutheran Publishing House of South Australia, 1975), 186.

15 Kenneth Heinitz (a former student of Martin Franzmann), conversation, November 1992.

16 Karl Rutz, "Ha! Ha! Among the Trumpets," *Response* 17, no. 1, 1977, p. 36.

17 Peter Franzmann, interview, August 1992.

18 Kenneth F. Korby, "Notes from the Editors Notebook," *The Cresset* 40 (November/ December 1976): 4–5.

19 Martin H. Franzmann, "O Kingly Love, That Faithfully," *Worship Supplement*, 757.

2

The Hymn Translations
and the Original Hymns

FRANZMANN'S REFLECTIONS ON CHRISTIAN
HYMNS AND POETRY

"Theology is Doxology. Theology must sing." [1]

With these words Martin Franzmann once began a sermon (based on Colossians 3:16) for Reformation Sunday. In these words he speaks volumes about his own life, work, and in particular, his approach to the song of the church. Theology is of no value if it does not bring us to the feet of our Lord in adoration, thanksgiving, and praise—

> Rather let the Word of Christ dwell in us richly, and then we shall find, sing, and produce the best song. We must produce. The song of the church must be an unending song. The church must cherish the best, but its song should not be a mere repetition of the song in the past. Then shall we sing with grace, with all emphasis on God and a most unsentimental subordination of ourselves. We shall sing to the Lord. With our song we shall guide one another continually to the center and fountain of the Christian's life and thus really teach and admonish one another. We shall see and then realize the ideal of all Christian song: the whole man with all his powers, with all his skills and gifts that God has bestowed upon him wholly bent on giving utterance to the peace that rules within him, wholly given to the purpose of letting the Word of Christ that dwells in him richly become articulate and audible through him to the upbuilding of the church and the glory of God. Then shall our theology become doxology. Then shall we sing with Mary: "My soul doth magnify the Lord, and my spirit hath rejoiced in God, my Saviour. . . . For He that is mighty hath done great things for me, and holy is His name." Amen. [2]

34

Franzmann was a man graced by God with many talents, but at heart he was a poet. It is evident from reading his writings, particularly his sermons and devotional writings, that the song of poetry, God's song, was in his heart. Often, when making a point on this or that, he would turn to poetry to make his meaning clear. Even when he quotes Scripture, he seems drawn to those parts of the Bible that are poetic in nature.

If our theology is to be doxology, then it must also be our best. Franzmann wanted no part of the everyday, sentimental poetry which, unfortunately, is so common in our churches today. In their mad rush to be "relevant," to reach the person in the pew "at his our her musical or poetic level," to "give them what they want to hear," our churches often cast out the pearls of the church's song for the gaudy trinkets of our modern age. This is a style which is like a river that runs a mile wide but is only a few inches deep. On this subject he writes—

> . . . And as we survey all hymnody we must acknowledge that the Holy Spirit worked not only in the Reformation but in all times and in all places in the one Christian and apostolic church, that in the best of what the Christian poets and Christian music makers have produced the church possesses so vast a store of the absolutely excellent that it need never stoop to substitutes.

> And yet there has always been a terrible fascination in *Ersatz*, especially for a sick church, a church grown so languid that it cannot bear to live in the last days. And so we have, instead of the full throated, joyful noise unto the Lord, the picture of the weary church sitting in a padded pew, weeping softly and elegantly into a lace handkerchief.

> And the amazing thing is how eloquent men can grow in defense of this shoddy *Ersatz* hymnody. They begin by criticizing the good hymns as "hard to sing." One might ask in return, Why must a hymn be easy? Who ever said it should be easy? Look at the wood cut of Albrecht Duerer's scene from the Apocalypse in which those that came from the great tribulation, who have washed their robes in the blood of the Lamb, sing their heavenly song. Look at those faces, their intensity of concentration, faces almost contorted with the energy of their devotion, if you would

35

know what singing with grace in your hearts to the Lord really means.

The fact that there is an amazing agreement on the part of hymnodists and musicians in all parts of the church as to what constitutes a good hymn counts for little with these critics. The hymnodist's passion for perfection is viewed with suspicion, as a sort of snobbery, and is usually countered with, "I don't know much about it, but I know what I like." That is really the ultimate snobbery. To pit my piping, squeaking little ego against all the good gifts God has given His church! It is worse than snobbery; it is ingratitude. It is as though God led us out into His great, wide world and showed us ripe, waving fields of grain and said to us, "Here is bread, and all for you." It is as though God had shown us cattle on a thousand hills and said to us, "Here is milk and cheese and butter and meat for you" and we replied, "No thanks! It is not to my taste. I'd rather go to a messy, dusty, fly-infested county fair and eat cotton candy."

Another argument might be called the "tin whistle" argument. Its essence is something like this: "After all, a man can make music on a tin whistle to the glory of God, and God will be pleased to hear it." True, true, true—if God has given us nothing more than a tin whistle; but God has given us infinitely much more. When He has given us all the instruments under heaven with which to sing His praises, then the tin whistle is no longer humility but a perverse sort of pride.

Perhaps the most insidious attack is the one that says: "Yes, these hymns are inferior, but we must use them as stepping stones to something better. We must use them to train people for the solid food of our best hymnody." I am reminded of a little poem on an artist who sold himself out, a poem not nearly as funny as it sounds:

> He found a formula for drawing comic rabbits,
> And the formula for drawing comic rabbits paid,
> But in the end he could not change the habits
> That the formula for drawing comic rabbits made.

We had better be careful about indulging in such condescensions, lest we too find the comic rabbits too powerful for us.[3]

In 1946 Franzmann wrote a series of four articles on Christian poetry that appeared in the *Northwestern Lutheran*. In these articles he was seeking to "win a wider audience for Christian poetry."[4] He began by defending poets in general against what he termed the two great prejudices of modern times: the ordinary reader's bias against poets generally, and the bias against Christian poetry specifically. In the balance of the four articles he then gave examples of what he felt were excellent pieces of Christian poetry: the anonymous 16th century "God Be in My Head"; John Donne's (1572–1631) "A Hymn to God the Father"; Sir Walter Raleigh's (1522–1618) "His Pilgrimage" (1603) and "The Conclusion" (1618); and finally George Herbert's (17th century) "Virtue." It is instructive to read what Franzmann had to say about poetry in general and Christian poetry in particular since it sheds light on his understanding of these and the manner in which he, in succeeding years, composed his own poems and hymns.

Christian poetry may be very simple as in "God Be in My Head" of which Franzmann writes:

> Much great poetry, like much great prose, is complicated and difficult; but great poetry, secular or Christian, need not be either. And the first evidence that I offer for the Christian poet is simplicity itself. "God Be in My Head" is anonymous and of the sixteenth century; it first appeared in the *Sarum Primer*. It is a prayer based on the thought of John 14:23— "If a man love me, he will keep my words; and my Father will love him, and we will come unto him, and make our abode with him;" a prayer that God may be in our every thought, look, word, and desire; that He may in full reality make His abode with us; and that He may be with us still when thinking, looking, speaking, and desiring cease, even in the hour of death. It is an elemental fact in Christian life, and elementally put; perhaps that is why it speaks so directly and strongly to us still, after four hundred years. [5]

But Christian poetry need not be only simple. In the second article Franzmann speaks of poetry which has greater formality and complexity. Here he refers to Donne's poem of which he writes:

> . . . in John Donne's "Hymn to God the Father" we are dealing with poetry of a different order, something more formal and complex, an elaborately and skillfully woven texture of great beauty and endowed with a somber splendor. This does not mean

that John Donne was at all less sincere than the unknown author of "God Be in My Head": a man may be elaborately or simply sincere, accordingly as God happens to have made him or the mood happens to be on him; some of the inspired psalms, for instance, are marvels of technical ingenuity, while others are simple both in language and in structure. If poetry is as wide as mankind, it is also as various.[6]

Sir Walter Raleigh in his long life was a statesman, courtier, soldier, explorer, historian, and poet. Twice in his life, first in 1603 and again in 1618, he faced the executioner's sharp blade. On the first occasion he wrote "His Pilgrimage" and on the second "The Conclusion." In both of these poems his strong faith and sure confidence of Heaven shine through the lines of the poems. Of these poems Franzmann says:

> At that time (1603) he had written a remarkable poem entitled "His Pilgrimage," full of vigorous and daring imagery and breathing a sure confidence of Heaven that is bracing to read. I quote a few lines of it as preface to "The Conclusion" to show how specifically his hope of heaven is centered in Christ: at the close of "His Pilgrimage" Raleigh pictures himself and the other pilgrims to Eternity as entering heaven's high judgement hall, where "Christ is King's Attorney, who pleads for all, without degrees." And then follow these splendid lines:
>
> > And when the grand twelve million jury
> > Of our sins, with direful fury,
> > Against our souls black verdict give,
> > Christ pleads His death, and then we live . . .
> > Of death and judgment, heaven and hell,
> > Who oft doth think, must needs die well.[7]

Franzmann apparently admired George Herbert and also the generation from which Herbert came because he says, "George Herbert belonged to the seventeenth century, that remarkable period in English history when every second Englishman was a poet and every third Englishman was a good poet."[8] Franzmann also notes that, influenced by his mother and the poet John Donne, Herbert turned to the religious life and lived out his days as a clergyman in the Church of England. Of the poem "Virtue" Franzmann writes:

The poem "Virtue" is one that is found in all anthologies; perhaps because it is, apparently, not specifically Christian and therefore inoffensive. I say "apparently"; for to those who know Herbert from his poems, from the prayers which he composed, from the testimony of his friends, and from the record of his life, the idea that the virtue spoken of in this poem is anything but virtue in Christ is simply preposterous. . . .

"Virtue" is a good example of the poet's way of saying things, of what is, not very aptly, called "poetic diction." For it is not only a way to say things, a way that irritates some honest people because it seems so indirect and roundabout; it is a way of communicating wholly different from that of simply saying things in prose. The poet desires, not merely to tell us what has moved him, but to have us re-create for ourselves, by our own activity of mind and imagination, the experience he has had. And to effect this he uses images, pictures, that our mind can take up and re-create, so that we enter actively into the beauty, or sorrow, or splendor that has stirred him.

So in the poem before us, Herbert would have us feel all the beauty that smote him on his morning walk, beauty that by its own loveliness reminded him of its transience, its liability to change, decay, death. He calls the day a "bridal" marriage, the perfect union of earth and sky; our mind gathers up all the impressions of good cheer, kindly feelings, youthful beauty, and hopeful love that cluster round the "bridal" idea and so constructs a warm and pulsing picture of the beauty of the morning.[9]

The balance of this chapter will be devoted to the original hymns and hymn translations of Martin Franzmann. The list includes nine translations and 13 original hymns. Most of these hymns and translations have appeared in print at various times over the past 58 years. Many of them have been published in modern hymnals of mainline church bodies. Every effort has been made to secure the oldest example of the text known to exist. In one case the total hymn had to be assembled from several sources.

THE HYMN TRANSLATIONS

THY STRONG WORD

Rise Again, Ye Lion-Hearted

1   Rise again, ye lion-hearted
Saints of early Christendom!
Whither is your strength departed
Whither gone your martyrdom?
　　Lo, love's light is on them,
　　Glory's flame upon them,
And their will to die doth quell
E'en the Lord and Prince of Hell!

2   These the men by fear unshaken,
Facing danger dauntlessly;
These no witching lust hath taken,
Lust that lures to vanity.
　　Mid the roar and rattle
　　Of tumultuous battle
In desire they soar above
All that earth would have them love.

3   Great of heart, they know no turning,
Honor, gold they laugh to scorn,
Quench desires within them burning,
By no earthly passion torn.
　　Mid the lions' roaring
　　Songs of praise outpouring,
Joyously they take their stand
On the arena's bloody sand.

4   Would to God that I might even
As the martyred saints of old,
With the helping hand of Heaven,
Steadfast stand in battle bold!
　　O my God, I pray Thee,
　　In the combat stay me!
Grant that I may ever be
Loyal knight and true to Thee!

© Text: "Lowen lasst euch wiederfinden," author unknown;
tr. Martin H. Franzmann
Tune: Bernard Klein, 1817

LOWEN LASST EUCH WIEDERFINDEN
87 87 66 77

Isaiah in a Vision Did of Old

Isaiah in a vision did of old
The Lord of hosts enthroned on high behold:
His splendid train was wide outspread until
Its streaming glory did the Temple fill.
Above His throne the shining Seraphim
With six-fold wings did reverence unto Him:
With twain each Seraph hid his glorious face,
And twain about his feet did interlace,
And with the other twain he soared on high,
And one unto another thus did cry:
    "HOLY, HOLY, HOLY IS THE LORD OF HOSTS!
    HIS GLORY FILLETH ALL THE EARTH!"
The beams and lintels at their crying shook,
And all the house was filled with billowing smoke.

© Text: Martin Luther, 1526; tr. Martin H. Franzmann
Tune: Martin Luther, 1526

JESAIA, DEM PROPHETEN
PM

Christ, Our Lord, Arose

1   Christ, our Lord, arose,
    Ended all His woes,
    Sing we then with heart and voice,
    In Christ our comforter rejoice.
       Kyrieleison!

2   Had death gained the victory,
    We all had perished utterly,
    Since our Lord is risen again,
    O sing His praise, ye sons of men.
       Kyrieleison!

3   Alleluia! Alleluia! Alleluia!
    Sing we then with heart and voice,
    In Christ our comforter rejoice.
       Kyrieleison!

Text: "Christ ist erstanden," 12th century, author unknown;
    tr. Martin H. Franzmann
Tune: Composer unknown

CHRIST IST ERSTANDEN
PM

The Dawn Has Driven Dark Night Away

1   The dawn has driven dark night away:
    Bestir you, brethren, rise and pray,
      Serve the Lord, your Master!

2   The Angel host forevermore
    With songs of praise their God adore,
      Lord of all creation.

3   The little birds and chanticleer
    Do praise their God with pipings clear
      Who doth clothe and feed them.

4   The sea, the earth, the golden sky
    Their Lord do laud and magnify
      Waiting on His pleasure.

5   After his kind each living thing
    That moves on earth or soars on wing
      Praiseth his Creator.

6   Thou man, so wonderfully made,
    With gifts so multifold arrayed,
      Drowsiness shake from thee!

7   God in His image hath thee made,
    His love and power to thee displayed,
      That thou mightest know Him.

8   That having tasted of His grace,
    And felt the radiance of His face,
      Thou shouldest love and praise Him.

9   Then rouse thee, diligently pray,
    Be faithful found, - mayhap today
      God may come to call thee.

10   In thought and deed be faithful found,
    Thy servant tongue His praise resound,
      Thank Him for His favor!

11   Pray thou the Father: "Thanks to Thee,
    That art from all eternity,
      For Thy bounteous blessings,

THY STRONG WORD

12 Through Jesus Christ, unto Whose praise,
    As unto Thee, the angels raise
        Voice and song in heaven.

13 And as they praise Thee, Lord, may I
    Henceforth to all eternity
        Ever praise Thee. Amen."

Text: "Der Tag vertreibt die Finster nach," Michael Weisse, 1480–1534;   DER TAG VERTREIBT DIE FINSTER NACH
    tr. Martin H. Franzmann   886
Tune: Michael Weisse, 1531

Jesus, Only, Naught But Jesus

1 Jesus, only, naught but Jesus
  Be my goal and longing still:
 Hear the pledge, Lord, that I make Thee,
  Evermore to do Thy will:
 For my heart which Thou hast filled
 Ever cries: "Lord, as Thou wilt!"

2 'Tis for Him that I am living,
  He alone my love shall be:
 Unto Jesus I am giving
  What in love He gave to me:
 Jesus' blood for me was spilt,
 Lord, O lead me as Thou wilt!

3 Take from me my dearest pleasure,
  If that pleasure please not Thee,
 Give me, Lord, of Thine own treasure,
  Give me what may profit me.
 Make me Thine, O Jesus mild,
 As Thou wilt, Thine own dear child!

4 All my soul and being ever
  Make obedient to Thy will:
 Grant that always I endeavor
  Thy good pleasure to fulfill:
 As Thou diedst for me, may I
 As Thou wilt, Lord, gladly die.

5 Lord, with many another blessing
  Thou hast given Thyself to me:
 Let me then with praise unceasing
  Sing the burden joyfully:
 Thou my life dost guard and shield,
 Lead me, Lord, e'en as Thou wilt!

Text: "Jesus, Jesus, nichts als Jesus," Ludaemille Elisabeth, Countess of Schwarzburg-Rudolstadt, 1640–72; tr. Martin H. Franzmann
Tune: Hamburg, 1715

JESUS, JESUS, NICHTS ALS JESUS
87 87 77

Praise Thou the Lord, My Soul, Praise and Adore Him

1   Praise thou the Lord, my soul, praise and adore Him,
While pulse and breath and being last:
Ever with laud and praise coming before Him,
I'll sing my God till life be past:
Thou God who hast created me
Both soon and late shalt praised be!
Alleluia! Alleluia!

2   Princes are dust, unto dust returning,
Of woman born, of man begot:
All their attemptings shall fade past discerning:
Yea, and their place shall know them not.
Since man can help thee not, nor stead,
Call thou on God when great thy need!
Alleluia! Alleluia!

3   Blessed, thrice blessed the man who hath taken
The God of Jacob for his own,
Who in the faith e'er abideth unshaken,
And trusteth in Christ alone:
Who trusts in God, on Him relies,
His hand is sure, his counsels wise!
Alleluia! Alleluia!

4   Heaven and earth, they are His creations,
His hand it is that made the sea.
He hath kept truth unto all generations,
The Champion of the oppressed is He.
The hungry man by Him is fed,
By Him the prisoner ransomed.
Alleluia! Alleluia!

5   Ways of the wicked the Lord overturneth
In pride's despite, despite renown:
But for the righteous the heart of Him burneth;
He raiseth them that are bowed down.
Then sing His praise, O shout again
His name Who shall forever reign!
Alleluia! Alleluia!

Text: "Lobe den Herren, o Meine Seele,"   LOBE DEN HERREN, O MEINE SEELE
   Johann Daniel Herrnschmidt, 1675–1723; tr. Martin H. Franzmann   10 8 10 8 88 8
Tune: Seelenharfe, Ansbach,1664

O Lord, We Praise Thee, Bless Thee and Adore Thee

O Lord, we praise Thee, bless Thee and adore Thee,
    Giving thanks, we bow before Thee,
That with Thy blood and body Thou hast fed us,
    May Thy gift, Lord, well bestead us!
        Kyrie Eleison!
O Thou Virgin-born, our Saviour Lord,
By Thy body broken, Thy blood outpoured,
      As in life, so in death
      Be Thou He that succoureth!
        Kyrie Eleison!

Text: "Gott sei gelobet und gebenediet," unknown 13th century;   GOTT SEI GELOBET UND GEBENEDIET
   tr. Martin H. Franzmann   PM
Tune: German melody, c. 1400

To Songs of Joy Awake Thee

1   To songs of joy awake thee,
       My heart, O rise, behold
   What light hath dawned to take thee
       From pain and darkness cold.
   My Saviour had Him laid
       Upon that final bed,
   Whereunto we must come,
       The cold and silent tomb.

2   The depths of hell rejoiced,
       The foes dark jubilee,
   Deep-throated, myriad-voiced,
       Proclaimed the victory,
   But ris'n in hell's despite
       Forth flashed in garments bright
   Our Champion, on the grave,
       To plant his banner brave.

3   Triumphant He ascendeth
       To realms beyond the sky;
   And wither my Lord wendeth
       Triumphant follow I;
   For this I know full well,
       By no proud prince of hell,
   By none of woman born
       Shall I be from Him torn.

4   Nor fear nor doubt shakes me,
       I follow calm and bold;
   To Heaven's high gate He takes me
       Wherein is writ in gold:
   "Since thou on earth hast borne
       For Me rebuke and scorn,
   Since thou hast died with Me,
       Here shalt thou crowned be."

Text: "Auf, auf, mein Herz, mit Freuden," Paul Gerhardt, 1648;
   tr. Martin H. Franzmann
Tune: Johann Crüger, 1648

AUF, AUF, MEIN HERZ
76 76 66 66

With High Delight Let Us Unite

1 With high delight let us unite
In songs of great jubilation.
Ye pure in heart, all bear your part,
Sing Jesus Christ, our Salvation.
To set us free forever, He
Is risen and sends to all earth's ends
Good news to save every nation.

2 True God, He first from death has burst
Forth into life, all subduing.
His Enemy vanquished doth lie;
His death has been death's undoing.
"And yours shall be like victory
O'er death and grave," saith He, who gave
His life for us, life renewing.

3 Let praises ring; give thanks, and bring
To Christ our adoration.
His honor spread by word and deed
To every land, every nation.
So shall His love give us above,
From misery and death set free,
All joy and full consolation.

© Text: "Mit Freuden zart," Georg Vetter, 1536–99; tr. Martin H. Franzmann
Tune: *Trente quarte pseaumes de David,* Geneva, 1551

MIT FREUDEN ZART
448 448 44 44 8

Among the translations done by Franzmann, there are a group of six that can be traced to his years at St. Peter's in Shaker Heights outside of Cleveland, Ohio. The congregation and its pastor, Arthur Katt, thought so highly of his work that they published the six translations along with one original hymn in December 1934.

Arthur Katt was probably the one most responsible for moving Franzmann toward the use of his talent for languages into the area of hymnody. Katt had a lifelong love for the hymnody of the church and became one of Franzmann's most outspoken proponents. In 1939 Katt put together his own independent analysis of the new hymnal (*The Lutheran Hymnal*, 1941), bound it, and sent it out to over a hundred select people in the Synodical Conference. Of Franzmann's abilities as a translator he writes:

> There is a man in the Synodical Conference, whose merits as poet and translator far surpass the attempts of all others in this direction. I refer to Professor Martin H. Franzmann, professor at Northwestern College, Watertown, Wis. While many others have tried their hand at this work, their products at best are but smooth, fluent prose rhymings,—metrically, rhythmically, mechanically correct. They do not soar. They reach no heights. I have yet to be shown one such hymn or translation which really approaches the exalted level of poetry, stirring the emotions, thrilling the worshipper with exalted beauty of thought and poetic expression.
>
> Quite different is the work of Martin H. Franzmann. I say this, not because Prof. Franzmann is my friend, but because his hymns have that certain something, which others lack.[10]

The first of the translations was "Rise Again, Ye Lion-Hearted" ("Lowen lasst euch wiederfinden," see p. 43). This was the only one of the early translations to be accepted by the Intersynodical hymnal committee for inclusion in the 1941 hymnal, a situation Katt decried at some length.

"Isaiah in a Vision Did of Old" ("Jesaia dem Propheten," see p. 44) was a second translation found in *Christian Hymns*. This one was given serious consideration for the 1941 hymnal. Both Katt and Franzmann were greatly disappointed that it was ultimately not chosen. Katt says the following:

. . . Again Franzmann's admirable translation, which Webber
(*The American Lutheran*, June 1937) praises so highly, outstrips
the proposed translation on every point.[11]

And Franzmann writes of the accepted translation:

The last line gives a wrong impression. "Smoke" is symbolic
of the Prayers of the Faithful ascending to God's throne. I can-
vassed the passage with some thoroughness, and found this to
be the interpretation. . . . I cannot conceive that the smoke is
meant to symbolize the presence of the Lord here, where He has
just been shown in enthroned splendor, filling the temple with the
glory of His train.[12]

Katt continues:

Franzmann's translation is simply majestic, brethren, as the
entire congregation of St. Peter's will testify.[13]

"Christ, Our Lord, Arose" (see p. 45) appeared as the first hymn
in *Christian Hymns* and is a translation of the 12th-century German hymn "Christ ist erstanden," which, according to Pollack, is
"the oldest German Easter hymn and one of the earliest German
hymns of any kind."[14] This too was offered to the hymnal committee, and it also was rejected. In regard to what actually appeared
in *The Lutheran Hymnal*, 1941, which was a translation done by
Pollack (*TLH* 187), Katt writes thus:

What the committee here offers us, is certainly devoid of all
merit. How much cheap ugliness is packed into those very few
lines! "Arisen" "death's painful prison" "rejoice with gladness" "end
all sadness" "ended" "ascended from the grave" "rejoice in gladness" "end all sadness" "Lord, have mercy!, Lord, have mercy!
Lord, have mercy!"!!!

What does Franzmann offer instead? He first objects to the
"mixed illustration": "Arisen from *prison*," used no doubt because
of the impossibility to find another word to rhyme with "arisen."
But that does not justify its employment. We arise from the dead;
we arise from the grave; but we do not arise from prison. We
escape from prison; we free ourselves from prison; we break out
of prison, etc.; but we do not arise from prison. Then again
Franzmann is of the opinion that "arisen" with its somewhat strident, light vowels would not sing so well on the rising slur, as
the deeper, more singable vowel "o" in "arose." So he was bold

enuf (sic) to employ the unusual past tense. Since the tune is Plainsong, it will adapt itself to the wording very well, even as it had to Luther's somewhat irregular meter.[15]

Katt regarded this next translation as one of the best Franzmann had done up to that time. "The Dawn Has Driven Dark Night Away," (see p. 46) a translation of Michael's Weisse's (1480–1534) "Der Tag Vertreibt die Finster Nacht," was the fourth hymn in *Christian Hymns*.

> In my estimation this is one of Franzmann's very best. My congregation has sung it many times, and regards it as a favorite. Luther called Michael Weisse "einen trefflichen deutschen Poeten" ["an excellent German poet"]; and this morning hymn is one of singular beauty. It is hidden away in the Anhang of the *Gesangbuch*. In Terre Haute my sainted father used it often, esp. for Saturday morning Catechumen instruction; he considered it a gem; taught us to appreciate it, and to find the frequent rhythmic inversions quaint and charming. The Germans will always remember it by its third stanza: "Die Haehn' und Voegel mancherlei." This stanza marks its uniqueness; the poet had the courage to depart from the commonplace "Fisch und Voegel," "birds and beasts," and introduce a particular kind of bird, a fowl, the cock, the rooster. At once the imagination was fired and captured; the children never forgot the "Haehn und Voegel mancherlei." Do you not see the beauty? Franzmann retained this unique feature, giving us "The little birds and chanticleer"; this again at once captured the imagination of the worshippers, the children in particular, in our Parish School. The term had to be explained to them once, to be sure, but after that they had won new friends: "the little birds and chanticleer." I have heard many adults likewise admit the same fascination for this term "chanticleer." Like with Weisse, so with Franzmann, this line "The little birds and chanticleer" at once marks the hymn, and sets it aside from others. And strange to say, it was this very term "chanticleer," so beautifully poetic, which one of the Committee members thought might prove objectionable.[16]

Katt goes on to point out that the children at St. Peter's School memorized the hymn of 13 short stanzas in very little time, a situation he regarded as "always a good sign."[17] Katt goes on to say the following:

Note the smooth flow from stanza to stanza, and the drive which increases as the hymn progresses, passing in review the various creatures of God, reaching its climax in the five stanzas beginning with "Thou man"! Note too the brilliant close, the prayer with its cleverly constructed doxology, revealing the masterly touch esp. in the second stanza!

What the Committee is substituting, "The shades of night have passed away," we have no way of telling, for this morning hymn has been placed in the Carol section, where it does not belong. The words have not been published; only the first line. To pass up Franzmann's unsurpassable translation is to be blind to beauty and poetry. To tamper with Franzmann's translation, giving it a revised beginning, is to be deaf to all warnings.[18]

"Jesus only, naught but Jesus" (see p. 48) appears fifth in *Christian Hymns*, 1934. This translation was a reworking of August Crull's 1880 translation of the hymn "Jesus, Jesus, nichts als Jesus" by Ludamilia Elisabeth, 1687. The Committee that worked on the 1941 hymnal adopted an altered version of Crull's original found in the 1931 revision of the 1919 hymnal. The 1919 edition had the third stanza:

> Seems a thing to me a treasure,
> Which displeasing is to Thee,
> Then remove such dangerous pleasure,
> Give instead what profits me. (Hymnal 1919)

Katt regarded this as being "smooth and grammatical."[19] But the 1931 edition of the hymnal altered the text to read:

> What to me may seem a treasure,
> Which displeasing is to Thee,
> Then remove such harmful pleasure,
> Give instead what profits me.

Of this change Katt writes:

> This, of course, not only needlessly alters Crull, but spoils his sentence structure to the point, where it is no longer grammatical. And all over Crull's name, as tho (sic) he were responsible for such botched-up English; with no indication of alteration. The low sneaking tamperer who is responsible for this and other like atrocities ought to be publicly reprimanded. Synodical officials should exercise vigilance that no one thus lay unholy hands on our hymns from one printing to another! Such tamperings in

the past can always be detected by the employment of lighter type by the printer, if you look closely.[20]

This hymn was a source of great consternation to both Katt and Franzmann which led to Franzmann retranslating the entire hymn. It is interesting to note Franzmann's own comments, as recorded by Katt, on this hymn. (Crull's translation found in the 1931 revision of the 1919 hymnal is given to aid the reader. Compare Franzmann's translation given on p. 48)

Although Crull has produced many admirable translations of the German hymns, we feel that this translation is one of his less happy efforts. To go into detail:

Stanza 1, Line 1: Threefold "Jesus, Jesus, Jesus" somewhat harsh (Rah, Rah, Rah effect)

Line 3: Oversentimental, no warrant in original

Line 4: "will"—ungrammatical

1 Jesus, Jesus, only Jesus,
    Can my heartfelt longing still.
    Without Him my soul is lonely,
    And I wish what Jesus will.
    For my heart, which He hath filled,
    Ever cries, Lord as Thou wilt.

Stanza 2, Line 1: "I'm living"

Line 2: "I'm loving"

Line 3: "I'm giving" Construction "I'm" is colloquial, in revivalistic manner

2 One it is for whom I'm living,
    Whom I'm loving faithfully;
    Jesus, unto whom I'm giving
    What in love He gave to me.
    Jesus' blood hides all my guilt;
    Lord, O lead me as Thou wilt.

Stanza 3, Lines 1–3: Crull's original: passable; revision destroys concinnity: "what" of line 1, left hanging in air; line 3 continues with "then," which presupposes an entirely different

> type of subordinate clause. Should by no
> means be allowed to stand.

3 What to me may seem a treasure
   But displeasing is to Thee,
   Then remove such harmful pleasure;
   Give instead what profits me.
   Let my heart by Thee be stilled;
   Make me Thine, Lord, as Thou wilt

Stanza 4, Line 3: "In me, through me, with me ever":
unhappy attempt to reproduce the German
angularity in English.

Line 5: "On Thee built": does not reproduce the
German "Ebenbild"

4 Grant that always I endeavor
   Thy good pleasure to fulfil;
   In me, through me, with me, ever,
   Lord, accomplish Thou Thy will.
   Let me die, Lord, on Thee built,
   When, and where, and as Thou wilt.

Stanza 5, Line 3: "And besides so many a blessing":
smacks of the German immigrant.

Line 5: "My Shield": abrupt introduction
of figure, harsh in English.[2]

5 Lord, my praise shall be unceasing,
   For Thou gav'st Thyself to me,
   And besides so many a blessing,
   That I sing now joyfully:
   Be it unto me, my Shield,
   As Thou wilt, Lord, as Thou wilt.

Katt then continues in praise of Franzmann's translation:

> How smoothly it reads! How gloriously it sings!

> How noble and chaste in expression! Nothing noisy and
> "polter"ing! (sic) Notice the use of "burden" in the sense of
> refrain, repeated theme! What a pleasure for the children to
> memorize![22]

The final translation found in Christian Hymns is that of Johann
Daniel Herrnschmidt's (1675–1723) hymn "Lobe den Herrn, o meine

Seele" or "Praise Thou the Lord, My Soul, Praise and Adore Him."
Christian Hymns contains the first three stanzas with the remaining
two found in Katt's Critical Comments on the Proposed New Hymnal. The original hymn consisted of seven stanzas. When Franzmann
made his translation, he condensed Herrnschmidt's stanzas 4, 5, 6,
and 7 into two stanzas numbered 4 and 5. (See p. 49 for the text of
the hymn.) Of this translation Katt says the following:

> Here you have a translation that is really worthy of the great hymn
> and its noble tune. Here is poetry, moving and lofty. You have
> here an example of the freedom Franzmann employs, and of
> which Dr. Dearmer says: "Perhaps it is true that translations fail
> when they seek to be literal thru ingenuity, and only triumph
> when they are free" . . . This freedom and faithfulness in (sic: are?)
> particularly evident in the treatment of the first two lines. Notice
> the clever use of scripture in line four, quite in keeping with the
> author's general idea, yet not directly suggested by him. Franz-
> mann's manner of translation is reminiscent of the high and noble
> work of Neale and Bridges.[23]

Katt notes Franzmann's careful use of vowels in relation to the
tune to which the hymn is sung. Singability was one of Franzmann's
concerns as he made his translations. He used "deep, round vowels on prominent or slurred final notes" rather than "strident, light
vowels choked with consonants."[24]

Katt also provides two additional early hymn translations by
Franzmann not found in *Christian Hymns.* The first of these is a sin-
gle stanza, an alternate translation to the first stanza of "Gott sei
gelobet und gebenedeit" or "O Lord, We Praise Thee, Bless Thee
and Adore Thee" (see p. 50). The Intersynodical Committee that
worked on *The Lutheran Hymnal* (1941) had dropped this hymn
but later decided to include it in the hymnal. Franzmann felt that the
first stanza was a poor translation and offered his translation as an
alternative to the committee. This hymn was a personal favorite of
Franzmann and he felt a strong need to express its post-Communion
joy in English.[25] Some elements of Franzmann's translation were
incorporated into the 1941 hymnal, especially the first line which
was certainly an improvement over the 1931 hymnal's "May God
be praised henceforth and blest forever."

"To Songs of Joy Awake Thee" (p. 51) is the other translation
found in Katt's work *Critical Comments on the Proposed New Hym-*

nal. The version used in the hymnal of 1931 contained lines that both Katt and Franzmann thought were of inferior quality. Katt writes:

> The old translation had some bad lines. The omnipresent, unescapable (sic) "gladness-sadness" rhyme, which so loves to push itself into prominence on special occasions and high feast days, made bold to occupy the very first line. This the revision did not change.
>
> Other bad lines: "They in the grave did sink Him"; which the revision has removed.
>
> "And waveth toward the skies His banner"; which the revision did not improve, but weakened still more: "His banner He doth wave, Triumphant o'er the grave" Waving of a banner: simply can not be done in English with dignity. It remains too much of College rooters.
>
> "Upon the grave is standing The Hero, looking round" These bad lines have been retained in the form: "Lo, on the tomb is standing The Hero, looking 'round."
>
> Do you see now, why F. R. Webber could speak of being "depressed at the prospect of singing our wretched translation 'Awake, My Heart, with Gladness,'" and why he was so overjoyed with Franzmann's translation? Franzmann has condensed the hymn, attempting to reproduce Gerhardt's thoughts in four stanzas.[26]

This translation also was published by F. R. Webber, the editor of "The Fine Arts in the Service of the Church," in *The American Lutheran* in June 1937. He had gone to Franzmann several years prior to the time of the article's publication with his concern over the existing translation of Gerhardt's hymn.

Within a few days Franzmann had provided him with a new translation. Webber writes of Franzmann's efforts:

> Our readers ought to know more about Pastor Katt's long and scholarly labors, as well as that astonishing genius, Professor Martin Franzmann, a highly gifted young clergyman of the Wisconsin Synod, whose beautiful poetry and hymn translations will compare with the great masters of classical English. Franzmann may well be called the Tennyson of the Lutheran Church. Two or three years ago, when depressed at the prospect of singing

our wretched translation "Awake, My Heart, with Gladness," the writer of these lines went to Prof. Franzmann with our troubles. Within a few days he gave us a translation that is not only beautiful as poetry, faithful to the original text, but which sings gloriously. We have used it during three Easter seasons.[27]

The last of Franzmann's translations is the one that he did many years after his first efforts in the 1930s. "With High Delight Let Us Unite" appeared in the *Worship Supplement* (1969). The hymn also was printed in the April 1, 1973 edition of *The Lutheran Witness* with what would appear to be Franzmann's original capitalization. It is this version of Franzmann's text that appears on p. 52

Georg Vetter's (1536–99) hymn "Mit Freuden zart" had not appeared in any of the earlier Lutheran hymnals in English, so Franzmann's translation was a new addition to the body of hymnody in the English language.

THE ORIGINAL HYMNS

Thou Art the Christ, the Son of the Living God

1   Though wisdom all her skills combine
To prove Thee man and only man,
Still doth Thine ancient glory shine,
Begotten ere all worlds began:
    Thou art the Christ, Thou art the God,
    Though in our ways Thy feet have trod.

2   I joy to own the mystery
That veils Thy birth from human ken:
Thy godhead there I chiefly see,
Where love hath made Thee Man of men:
    Thou art the Christ, Thou art the God,
    Though in our ways Thy feet have trod.

3   Th' uncomprehending sacrifice,
Thy bitter death upon the tree
O Christ, the God for man that dies,
Triumphant owns His deity:
    Thou art the Christ, Thou art the God,
    Though in our ways Thy feet have trod.

4   The Man into the grave was laid,
On Easter morn the God arose
O proof complete, divinely made:
He suffered death because He chose!
    Thou art the Christ, Thou art the God,
    Though in our ways Thy feet have trod.

5   Then praise to God the Father be,
His Saviour Son to us Who lent:
The Comforter be Praised, Whom He,
Th' ascended God, to us hath sent:
    Thou art the Christ, Thou art the God,
    Though in our ways Thy feet have trod.

© Text: Martin H. Franzmann, 1959
Tune: *Geistliche Lieder,* 1539

VATER UNSER
88 88 88

Thy Strong Word Did Cleave the Darkness

1 Thy strong word did cleave the darkness;
   At Thy speaking it was done;
   For created light we thank Thee,
   While Thine ordered seasons run:
       Alleluia! Alleluia!
   Praise to Thee who light dost send!
       Alleluia! Alleluia!
       Alleluia without end!

2 Lo, on men who dwelt in darkness,
   Dark as night and deep as death,
   Broke the light of Thy salvation,
   Breathed Thine own life-breathing breath:
       Alleluia! Alleluia!
   Praise to Thee who light dost send!
       Alleluia without end!
       Alleluia without end!

3 Thy strong word bespeaks us righteous;
   Bright with Thine own holiness,
   Glorious now, we press toward glory,
   And our lives and hopes confess:
       Alleluia! Alleluia!
   Praise to Thee who light dost send!
       Alleluia! Alleluia!
       Alleluia without end!

4 From the cross Thy wisdom shining
   Breaketh forth in conquering might;
   From the cross forever beameth
   All Thy bright redeeming light:
       Alleluia! Alleluia!
   Praise to Thee who light dost send!
       Alleluia! Alleluia!
       Alleluia without end!

THY STRONG WORD

5 Give us lips to sing Thy glory,
   Tongues Thy mercies to proclaim,
   Throats that shout the hope that fills us,
   Mouths to speak Thy holy name:
       Alleluia! Alleluia!
   May the light which Thou dost send
   Fill our songs with alleluias,
       Alleluias without end!

6 God the Father, Light Creator,
   To Thee laud and honor be;
   To Thee, Light of Light begotten,
   Praise be sung eternally;
   Holy Spirit, Light-Revealer
   Glory, glory be to Thee;
   Men and angels, now and ever
   Praise the Holy Trinity! Amen.

© Text: Martin H. Franzmann, 1954
Tune: Thomas J. Williams 1869–1944

EBENEZER
87 87 D

O Thou, Whose Fiery Blessing

1　O Thou whose fiery blessing can
　　Make pure the unclean lips of man;
　　That takest man and makest him
　　A singer with the seraphim;

2　O Thou that buildest mighty praise
　　From shouts that children's voices raise;
　　That canst, when human voices die,
　　Make silent stones to prophesy:

3　Oh, speak to us Thy potent Word,
　　That we may say, "Thus saith the Lord."
　　That in our frailty we may be
　　A wall of brass that echoes Thee.

© Text: Martin H. Franzmann, 1958
Tune: William Knapp, 1738

WAREHAM
LM

O Thou, Who Hast of Thy Pure Grace

1 O Thou, who hast of Thy pure grace
Made shine on us a Father's face,
Arise, Thy holy name make known;
Take up Thy power and reign alone;
On earth, in us, let Thy sole will
Be done as angels do it still.

2 O King and Father, kind and dread,
Give us this day our daily bread;
Forgive us, who have learned to bless
Our enemies, all trespasses;
Spare us temptation, let us be
From Satan set forever free.

3 Thine is the kingdom, unto Thee
Shall bow in homage every knee;
And Thine the power; no power shall be
That is not overcome by Thee;
The glory Thine, by every tongue
Thy praise shall be forever sung.

© Text: Martin H. Franzmann, 1959
Tune: *Geistliche Lieder*, 1539

VATER UNSER
88 88 88

In Adam We Have All Been One

1   In Adam we have all been one,
One huge rebellious man;
We all have fled that Evening Voice
That sought us as we ran.

2   We fled Thee and in losing Thee
We lost our brother too;
Each singly claimed and sought his own;
Each one his brother slew.

3   But Thy strong love, it sought us still
And sent us Thine only Son
That we might hear His Shepherd's voice
And, hearing Him, be one.

4   O Thou who, when we loved Thee not,
Didst love and save us all,
Thou great Good Shepherd of mankind,
O hear us when we call.

5   Send us Thy Spirit, teach us truth;
Thou Son, O set us free
From fancied wisdom, self-sought ways,
To make us one in Thee.

6   Then shall our song united rise
To Thine eternal throne,
Where with the Father evermore
And Spirit thou art One. Amen.

© Text: Martin H. Franzmann, c. 1961
Tune W. Walker, *Southern Harmony*, 1835

THE SAINTS'S DELIGHT
CM

Our Lord Has Laid His Benison

1 Our Lord has laid His benison
On all our human roots and ties,
On father, mother, daughter, son,
On all that laughs and cries.

2 No stranger to the wedding feast,
At Cana, when the wine was spent,
He largely gave, and gave the best,
For fam'ly merriment.

3 He bade the timid mothers bring
Their children to Him to be blessed,
And promised that for such the King
Is King above the rest.

4 He lived with us, He wept with us,
He knew our human pangs and fears.
When Mary wept for Lazarus,
He did not stay His tears.

5 E'en when He hung upon the cross,
Then at the last, when all was done,
He spoke to lessen Mary's loss:
"Woman, behold thy son!"

6 O Thou, who once in Thy sole death
Hast borne and buried all our sin
And by Thy life hast given breath
To all Thy ransomed kin,

7 Let all our ties of heart and mind
By Thy great love transfigured be,
And may these bonds be bonds that bind
Us each to each and Thee!

8 To God our Father through the Son
All glory, laud, and honor be,
And to the Spirit, with Them One,
Now and eternally.

Text: Martin H. Franzmann, 1963
Tune: Hugo Gehrke, 1963

88 86

O God, O Lord of Heaven and Earth

1   O God, O Lord of heaven and earth,
    Thy living finger never wrote
    That life should be an aimless mote,
    A deathward drift from futile birth.
    Thy word meant life triumphant hurled
    Through every cranny of Thy world.
    Since light awoke and life began,
    Thou hast desired Thy life for man.

2   Our fatal will to equal Thee,
    Our rebel will, wrought death and night.
    We seized and used in Thy despite
    Thy wondrous gifts of liberty.
    We housed us in this house of doom,
    Where death had royal scope and room,
    Until Thy Servant Prince of Peace
    Breached all its walls for our release.

3   Thou camest to our hall of death,
    O Christ, to breathe our poisoned air,
    To drink for us the dark despair
    That strangles man's reluctant breath.
    How beautiful the feet that trod
    The road that leads us back to God!
    How beautiful the feet that ran
    To bring the great good news to man!

4   O Spirit, who didst once restore
    Thy Church, that it might be again
    The bringer of good news to men,
    Breathe on Thy cloven church once more,
    That in these gray latter days
    There may be men whose life is praise,
    Each life a high doxology
    To Father, Son, and unto Thee.

©Text: Martin H. Franzmann
Tune: Richard Hiller, b. 1923
1966

MISSION
10 10 10 with alleluias

© Text: Martin
H. Franzmann,
WITTENBERG NEW

O Fearful Place, Where He Who Knows Our Heart

1 O fearful place where He who knows our heart
Lays bare our sins—O Lord, from us depart!
We cannot live where Thou, the Holy, art.
     Alleluia! Alleluia!

2 O House of God, where angel troops descend
     From heaven to man and on his saints attend;
Here let us sing the song that knows no end:
     Alleluia! Alleluia!

3 O gate of heaven, where God's almighty Word,
Big with forgiveness, constantly is heard,
And God's elect to shouts of praise are stirred:
     Alleluia! Alleluia!

4 O Son of God, who diedst our life to win,
Here in this house we died Thy death to sin,
And from the dead with these have raised been.
     Alleluia! Alleluia!

5 Thy servants here took our young life in hand
And taught us all that Thy love did command
And made us in Thy Spirit's strength to stand.
     Alleluia! Alleluia!

6 Thy body given and Thy blood outpoured
In bread and wine here we have tasted, Lord;
For this Thy gift forever be adored!
     Alleluia! Alleluia!

7 O God Almighty, gracious Three in One,
On this Thy house let praise to Thee be done
Until we join in heaven's high unison:
     Alleluia! Alleluia!

© Text: Martin H. Franzmann
Tune: Richard Hillert, b. 1923

MISSION
10 10 10 with alleluias

O Kingly Love, That Faithfully

1   O kingly Love, that faithfully
    Didst keep Thine ancient promises
    Didst bid the bidden come to Thee,
    The people Thou didst choose to bless,
        This day we raise
        Our song of praise,
        Adoring thee,
        That in the days
        When alien sound
        Had all but drowned
        Thine ancient, true, and constant melody,
        Thy mighty hand did make
        A trumpet none could silence or mistake;
        Thy living breath did blow for all the
                world to hear,
        Living and clear:
        The feast is ready - come to the feast,
        The good and the bad,
        Come and be glad,
        Greatest and least,
        Come to the feast!

2   O lavish Love, that didst prepare
    A table bounteous as Thy heart,
    That men might leave their puny care
    And taste and see how good Thou art,
        This day we raise . . .

3   O seeking Love, Thy hurrying feet
    Go searching still to urge and call
    The bad and the good on every street
    To fill Thy bounteous banquet hall.
        This day we raise . . .

4   O holy Love, Thou canst not brook
    Man's cool and careless enmity;
    O ruthless Love, Thou wilt not look
    On man robed in contempt of Thee.
        Thine echoes die;
        Our deeds deny
        Thy summoning:

THY STRONG WORD

Our darkling cry,
Our meddling sound
Have all but drowned
That song that once made every echo ring.
Take up again, O take
The trumpet none could silence or mistake,
And blow once more for all the world to
     hear,
Living and clear:
The feast is ready—come to the feast,
The good and the bad,
Come and be glad,
Greatest and least,
Come to the feast!

© Text: Martin H. Franzmann, 1966
Tune: Richard Hillert, b. 1923

KINGLY LOVE
PM

Weary of All Trumpeting

1 Weary of all trumpeting, weary of all killing,
 Weary of all songs that sing promise, non-ful-
  filling
 We would raise, O Christ, one song;
 We would join in singing that great music
  pure and strong,
 Wherewith heaven is ringing.

2 Captain Christ, O lowly Lord, Servant King,
  Your dying
 Bade us sheath the foolish sword, bade us
  cease denying.
 Trumpet with Your Spirit's breath through
  each height and hollow;
 Into Your self-giving death, call us all to fol-
  low.

3 To the triumph of Your cross summon all men
  living;
 Summon us to love by loss, gaining all in giving,
 Suffering all, that men may see triumph in surrender;
 Leaving all, that we may be partners in Your
  splendor.

© Text: Martin H. Franzmann
Tune: Hugo Distler, 1938

DISTLER
76 76 D

Thy Word Has Been Our Daily Bread

1 Thy Word has been our daily bread;
       We seek no food but Thine,
   Thy Word in Thine own lowliness,
       All human and divine.

2 The Word was found, and we did eat;
       Thy Word has made us be
   Thy servants bound to Thee in bonds
       More sweet than liberty.

3 We have Thy Word; Thy Word endures
       When all man's glory ends.
   The Word has promised we shall serve
       Not as Thy slaves, but friends.

4 Grant us the heart to heed Thy Word,
       Give us the strength to be
   Thy friends who serve, not duty bound,
       But free as Thou art free.

5 Then at Thy promise we shall go
       And plenteous fruit bring in;
   Thy teeming, fruitful years shall fill
       Thy Father's barn and bin.

6 When to the home Thou hast prepared
       At last we all shall come,
   To Father, Spirit, and to Thee
       We'll raise the harvest-home.

©Text: Martin H. Franzmann
Tune: Jeremiah Clarke, 1709
    William Croft, 1708

ST. MAGNUS or ST. ANNE
CM

O Thou, Who on Th' Accursed Ground

1 O Thou, who on th' accursed ground
Didst plant the blessing of Thy call,
Who to our father Abraham
Didst speak the word that promised all;

2 O Thou, who in Thy choosing love
Didst call Thine Israel to be
The royal people and Thy priests
To offer sacrifice to Thee;

3 O Thou, who from his grubby wealth
Didst once Thy servant Matthew call,
To leave that rubbish for Thy gold
To speak Thy word to nations all.

4 We thank Thee for the serving-men
By Thy redeeming word set free
For servitude, for bondage found
More sweet than selfish liberty.

5 We thank Thee for the men whose heart
Is freely open to Thy word,
Is freely moved to love all men
Who name and serve Thee as their Lord.

6 Ah, grant that they, and we, may stand
Before Thee when Thou com'st again
And by the glory of Thy grace
May share the glory of Thy reign.

© TextL Martin H. Franzmann
Tune: Donald Rotermund, 1974

LM

Preach You the Word

1 Preach you the Word and plant it home
    To men who like or like it not,
The Word that shall endure and stand
    When flow'rs and men shall be forgot.

2 We know how hard, O Lord, the task
    Your servants bade us undertake:
To preach Thy Word and never ask
    What prideful profit it may make.

3 The sower sows; his reckless love
    Scatters abroad the goodly seed,
Intent alone that men may have
    The wholesome loaves that all men need.

4 Though some be snatched and some be scorched
    And some be choked and matted flat,
The sower sows; he cries out,
    "Oh, what of that, and what of that?"

5 Preach you the Word and plant it home
    And never faint; the Harvest Lord
Who gave the sower seed to sow
    Will watch and tend His planted Word.

© Text: Martin H. Franzmann
Tune: *Rheinfelsisches Gesangbuch*, 1666

O HEILAND, REISS DIE HIMMEL AUF
LM

The Shaker Height's collection, *Christian Hymns*, in addition to the six hymn translations, also contained an original hymn by Franzmann entitled "Thou Art the Christ, The Son of the Living God" (see p. 65) based on the words of Peter recorded in Matthew 16:16. This hymn, also, was presented to the Intersynodical Committee for inclusion in *The Lutheran Hymnal*. Arthur Katt wrote of this hymn:

> Finally, we bring to your attention this fine tribute to the Saviour, extolling His deity and Messiahship, which fills a definite need in our day of Modernism. Every time I preach on the Deity of our Lord, I have the congregation sing this hymn. It is scholarly, noble, on a high poetic level. The more I sing it, the better I like it. It has become to me and my congregation a real treasure. Remember, it comes from a university bred man, assailed by all the doubts of modern learning. This is not a translation, but an original poem. Here you have real poetry, which must be studied. Many beauties lie hidden here; continued use reveals them more and more. Note the progression: Godhead from eternity, Incarnation, Depth of Humiliation, Atoning Death, Glorious Resurrection, all evidencing the Messiahship and Deity of the Man Christ Jesus! One of the outstanding fine features of this hymn is the constant five-fold repetition of the firm conviction:
>
> > Thou art the Christ, Thou art the God,
> > Though in our ways Thy feet have trod!
>
> the confession of certainty becoming stronger and stronger, as this growing conviction flows from the various aspects of the Lord's person and work, from the succeeding events in the God-man's life presented stanza for stanza. This refrain is literally sung into the worshippers' hearts. Even the little children who cannot read always repeat these last two lines.
>
> What striking beauty here, what fine poetry:
>
> > "The Man into the grave was laid,
> > On Easter morn the God arose!"
>
> This, of course does not mean a separation of the person of Christ; it does not mean, that He who was laid into the grave was not God, or that He who rose from the dead was not a man. Let us beware of dissecting poetry thus! The meaning is evident: Christ's death and burial prove His humanity; there we see Him from the

human side; Christ's resurrection, on the other hand, proves His deity; there we see Him from the divine side.

The entire hymn comes to a glorious close in one of the finest, most delicately constructed Doxologies, I have ever read, revealing the masterly touch of Franzmann's pen. Study the construction of the last stanza: how perfect, how complete!

The style here again is reminiscent of John Mason Neale and that of Robert Bridges, who constructed some beautiful doxologies. Thus the hymn comes to a brilliant close, firm conviction followed by an outburst of joy![28]

That Franzmann intended this hymn would be sung to the German hymn tune *Vater unser* is evidenced by Katt's additional comments.

One word about the tune. *Vater unser im Himmelreich* is a great favorite of the author and poet. He likes it immensely. The solidity appeals to him, the massiveness of the tune. . . . He deplored the fact, that, aside of Luther's paraphrase of the Lord's Prayer (which has nine stanzas and must be sung complete), we have no hymn for general use, that might serve as a carrier of this somewhat solemn Chorale tune. . . . This realization in part prompted him to write the above hymn. He wrote the words for the tune; or rather, he wrote the words with the tune in mind.[29]

The October 26, 1954 edition of *The Lutheran Witness* contained, tucked away on the inside front cover amidst the "Letters," four stanzas (1, 2, 3, and 5) of a new hymn based on the motto of the St. Louis Seminary "Light from Above." The hymn "Thy Strong Word Did Cleave the Darkness" was first sung by the student body of the Seminary at their morning chapel devotion on October 7, 1954, when Dr. Walter E. Buszin was the chapel speaker.[30] The hymn was included in the *Seminary Service Book* (1954) and contained five stanzas. Stanzas four and five, as found in the *Worship Supplement*, and as given on p. 66 of this text, were reversed in the service book.

It is clear that Franzmann intended this hymn, with the Welsh hymn melody *Ton-y-botel* (*Ebenezer*), to be a sort of "Seminary hymn." However, it was far too good a hymn to stay the private property of the seminary. Evidence of this hymn's great popularity is shown by the large number of modern hymnals that include it as

well as the number of composers who have made settings of this fine hymn.

The sixth stanza appears in the *Worship Supplement* and is considered by some to be among the finest, if not the finest doxology ever written in the Western Church. Bruce R. Backer, a professor at Luther College, New Ulm, Minnesota, writes:

> Most liturgical expression is at the same time doxological, since it is the Christian's chief duty in addressing God to thank and praise him especially for the great gift of salvation through Jesus Christ. Martin Franzmann penned perhaps the greatest doxology in the entire corpus of western hymnody (see *Worship Supplement* 747, stanza 6).[31]

Much good hymnody is doxological in character, that is, it is trinitarian. In addition to being doxological "Thy Strong Word" is also doctrinal. A good hymn weaves good theological content throughout all the stanzas, and, as we look at the hymns of Martin Franzmann, we find that this is the case. Backer goes into a bit of analysis of the hymn as follows:

> This hymn rejoices exceedingly in the grace of God, as he leads people from the darkness of unbelief to faith in God through Jesus Christ.
>
> 1. Stanza one uses Genesis 1:1–2 as a giant metaphor for the miracle of conversion from unbelief to faith. It also begins the six-fold Alleluia, which ends this and the succeeding three stanzas.
>
> 2. The second stanza now speaks of the new creation, 2 Corinthians 5:17. The light of salvation broke on men who dwelt in darkness. The Holy Spirit spoke the Word of the Gospel.
>
> 3. The third stanza begins with an excellent statement of forensic justification: "Thy strong word bespeaks us righteous." Dressed in the freely given righteousness of Christ we confess our hopes with the life we lead.
>
> 4. The fifth stanza offers a typical application according to the Psalter: speak the things that you have heard and seen. In today's action culture speech is often less important than getting something done. The Bible, however, considers witnessing the truth in Christ Jesus to be the firstfruit of the Gospel.

5. The last stanza is perhaps the greatest doxology in Christian hymnody.[32]

Franzmann wrote on the subject of God's powerful Word in an article with the title "Quick and Powerful" for the *Concordia Theological Monthly* in March 1951. In this article we see the doctrinal basis from which the hymn arises.

> As God is, so is His Word to us: quick and powerful. . . . the Gospel is a divine action and confronts and calls us into His grace. It is quick and powerful in virtue of the God who speaks it. We see it plainly in Jesus' answer to John the Baptist: "The blind receive their sight, and the lame walk, the lepers are cleansed, and the deaf hear, the dead are raised up, and the poor have the *Gospel preached* to them" (Matt. 11:5). The preaching of the Gospel is in a series of actions and is the climax of the series. The Word has power, it works and creates what it says: the Messianic age foretold by Isaiah has dawned. . . .

> The setting for our preaching of this Word is true to the nature of the proclamation as it ought to be. The liturgy moves; and for all its stately splendor is full of the lively tension that comes with the interaction between God's grace and the penitent and believing heart of man. The best of our hymnody, too, words and music, is a supple and vivid voicing of God's great redemptive action and man's response. . . .

> The Word is quick; we must let it live. The Word is powerful; we must let it work.[33]

Another hymn bears the title "O Thou, Whose Fiery Blessing" (see p. 68) and appeared in *The Lutheran Witness* in May 1958. The hymn contains three stanzas and bears the instruction that the hymn should be sung to the melody of hymn 608 in *The Lutheran Hymnal, Wareham.*

The imagery of the hymn reflects, in the first stanza, the cleansing of Isaiah's lips by the hot coal in the tongs held by the angel.

> O Thou, whose fiery blessing can,
> Make pure the unclean lips of man;

The second stanza calls to mind the Palm Sunday entry into Jerusalem where Jesus answers the protests over the children's song of "Hosanna" by declaring that if the children were silenced then the very stones would cry out in praise.

> O Thou that buildest mighty praise
> From shouts that children's voices raise;
> That canst, when human voices die,
> Make silent stones to prophesy:

This leads to the final stanza which sums up the previous two by pointing to the power of the Word of God to change our "frailty" to "A wall of brass that echoes Thee."

The *Seminary Service Book* (1959) contained another of Franzmann's hymns expressly written for the service book. The new hymn was titled "O Thou, Who Hast of Thy Pure Grace" (see p. 69) and was actually first published in the May 5, 1959 edition of *The Lutheran Witness*. It is a paraphrase of the Lord's Prayer after the manner of Luther's "Vater unser im Himmelreich," but having three rather than nine stanzas. Considering what Arthur Katt said about Franzmann's love for the hymn tune *Vater unser,* it is not surprising to find him writing his own paraphrase of the Lord's Prayer.

"In Adam We Have All Been One" (see p. 70) first appeared in print in 1967, in a collection of hymns entitled *A New Song.* The hymn dates from around 1961, when it may have been first sung on the St. Louis Seminary campus.[34] This is a hymn rich in doctrinal content regarding the Fall, original sin, and God's great love shown by the sacrifice of His Son for a depraved and lost humankind.

The genesis of this hymn can be traced in Franzmann's theological writing at least as far back as the 1949, Bad Boll Conferences in Europe where Franzmann presented a paper entitled "Augustana II: Of Original Sin" where he wrote:

> Since Adam's fall, then, the history of mankind outside Christ is the history of the growth and spread of sin. . . . Since Adam, and from Adam, the whole history of mankind is the history of sin, and the lot of mankind is that of enslavement to death and the devil . . . . For when the *Solid Declaration* says that "original sin is propagated from sinful seed, through carnal conception and birth from father and mother" (I, 7), it is not "explaining" the propagation of sin; rather, it is stating the community of guilt that is the lot of mankind since Adam in Biblically concrete (Psalm 51) terms. The center of gravity remains the inevitable present guilt, the present enslavement of mankind.

According to our Confessions every man and the whole of each man is a sinner. As a sinner, man is estranged from God. To be born *cum peccato* ["with sin"] means to be, first, *sine metu Dei, sine fiducia erga Deum* ["without the fear of God, without trust toward Him"]; more it means that man is *incapable* of the true fear of God, true trust in Him. . . .

Original sin is the lot or fate of man. Being born involves being a sinner. . . .

And this sin is real sin, real guilt; the tracing back of original sin back to Adam does not exonerate the sinner. The line does not run backwards from us to Adam, but forward from Adam to us, "so that we are by nature the children of wrath, death, and damnation, unless we are delivered by the merit of Christ." (*Solid Declaration* I, 5)[35]

Bruce Backer holds this hymn up as an example of what he terms "doctrinal expression," which he considers to be one of the requirements of a good hymn. Of the hymn he writes:

If liturgical hymnody recites to God the great things he has done in terms of the three articles of the Christian faith, then such expression will be doctrinal. By teaching, it will build the faith and life of the worshipping community of believers. The corpus of Lutheran hymnody, from Luther to the present, is especially rich in doctrinal content, in particular sin and grace: a person's total inability to please God and God's rescue mission through Jesus Christ, his one and only son. The doctrine of original sin is denied by many, outwardly confessed but inwardly denied by others, but joyously confessed by the Holy Christian Church, the community of beggars.

The biblical interpreter's hymns are bound to make use of the Word of God. In fact, in the case of Franzmann we say his hymns are saturated with biblical thought.

1. In Adam We Have All Been One
   a. The Fall
   b. The murder of Abel
   c. The Good Shepherd's voice[36]

Backer also writes:

Using the metaphor of the person, or body, the poet presents the comprehensiveness of original sin and the believers release from its grasp.

1. By evoking the picture of the rebellion in Eden and by using the pronoun "we," the poet presents the comprehensiveness of original sin "one huge rebellious man."

2. Rebellion against God works itself out in our social relationships. Adam and Eve rebelled against God. Their offspring committed fratricide. Moses intended the two stories to belong together and to be applied as a unit. The poet does it.

3/4. Jesus is presented as the only hope. He saves us through his Word, the voice. At the right hand of God Jesus still is the Shepherd of mankind, listening to the prayers of believers and interceding for them before the Father.

5. The Holy Spirit alone can set us free from the wisdom we create. He can turn us from the paths we have made for ourselves. Teach us truth, Holy Spirit![37]

The year 1963 was established as the year of the family and The Lutheran Church— Missouri Synod's service organization, the Lutheran Laymen's League, chose "God at Work in Christian Families" as their emphasis for 1963–64. Franzmann and Hugo Gehrke were commissioned by the Lutheran Laymen's League to produce a hymn for families. Gehrke produced the hymn tune while Franzmann provided the text. The result was "Our Lord Has Laid His Benison" (see p. 71) which the Lutheran Laymen's League published in a little pamphlet entitled "A Hymn for Families."

The hymn looks at families from a Biblical rather than a sentimental viewpoint. In stanza 1 the poet states that God's blessing (benison) is placed on all humankind in all our family relations whether immediate or extended. Stanza 2 points to Jesus at Cana's wedding feast and how He blessed that couple's festivities with the very best wine. Stanza 3 refers to the mothers bringing their children to Jesus for His blessing and how Jesus is the King of all His children. The story of Mary and Lazarus forms the background for stanza 4 where Jesus shows his humanity and His compassion for us even in our times of greatest sorrow and suffering. The crucifixion is pictured in stanza 5 where in His dying agony Jesus still cared for His mother by softening her loss through the disciple

John. Stanza 6 reminds of His care for our greatest need, the forgiveness of our sins which is extended to all within the circle of our families. Christian unity, which binds us all far closer than the ties of blood, is spoken of as a sharing of Christ's love with each other and with Him in stanza 7. The thought of this stanza is a continuation of that in stanza 6. That which binds us together, that love which is Christ's gift to us, is found, is rooted, in the cross of Calvary where He who loved with the greatest love freed us to love one another. The hymn then closes, as Franzmann liked to do, on a note of doxology.

> Then Christ shall have His glory full and whole when God is All in all; the close and conclusion of all eschatology, the end of all things, in the Son's act of adoration, His "subjection" to the Father, that intra-Trinitarian liturgy to which a redeemed mankind and a redeemed creation do all speak their loud and eternal "Amen."[38]

The year 1967 marked the 450th anniversary of the Reformation. Franzmann was commissioned to write a hymn in celebration of this historical milestone. This time he worked with composer Jan Bender who produced the tune *Wittenburg New*. The product on Franzmann's part was the hymn "O God, O Lord of Heaven and Earth" (see p. 72), which he completed somewhere around September 23, 1966.[39]

This hymn is one of doctrine: doctrine of the power of the Word; of original sin; of God's judgment on the sinner; of the Prince of Peace, the Redeemer and His vicarious atonement; of the power of the Spirit to bring to humanity the Word and to build the Church from such frail people as we; and of the Trinity to whom all believers live in a doxology of praise. It is a doctrinal hymn after the fashion of those of the Reformation period, calling to remembrance the great hymn of Martin Luther "Dear Christians One and All Rejoice" and its companion Paul Speratus's "Salvation Unto Us Has Come."

Of this hymn Bruce R. Backer writes:

> In this hymn the poet goes to war against nihilism, the philosophy that life has no meaning. He addresses Father, Son, and Holy Spirit to aid him in the struggle.

1. Father, you never wrote that our life is a mere speck, drifting aimlessly from meaningless birth to meaningless death. Your Word brought life, and it reveals that you spent yourself on our behalf.

2. We are rebels and have misused your precious gifts. Our life became a house of doom. But Jesus broke the walls and released us.

3. Our rebellion is like poisoned air that gradually strangles us. But the Good News frees us and brings us back to God.

4. Holy Spirit, bring us a fresh outpouring of Your Word that it may make our life a life of praise, "a high doxology to Father, Son, and unto Thee."[40]

Backer also criticizes this hymn as an example of what happens when a student of the classics writes hymns. Namely that some of the ideas and images may be foreign to the reader. He states that the concept of life without meaning is strange to those who have never studied philosophy. The words "mote" and "cranny" found in stanza 1, along with "Thy living finger," which represents the Holy Spirit, are thought to be too difficult. Backer also believes that the phrase "in Thy despite" offers difficulty because it is a noun form of a word, "despise," which is usually used as a verb.[41]

A hymn which first appeared in the *Worship Supplement* (1969) was "O Fearful Place, Where He Who Knows Our Hearts" (see p. 73). Franzmann's brother Werner believes that this hymn was originally written as a hymn for a church anniversary. He reasons this is so because of the reference in stanzas 1 and 2 to Jacob's vision of the ladder to heaven in Genesis 28:12.[42]

A close study of the text also reveals other references that make it clear that the poet is talking about the church. Stanza 1 refers to the Word, the Law, which cuts like a two-edged sword revealing our sinfulness and making us aware of our need for repentance and forgiveness. In stanza 2 it is also the place where all God's saints in heaven and on earth offer their worship and praise. The Gospel stands forth in stanza 3 with its constant message of forgiveness preached in the hearing of God's holy people. Stanza 4 speaks of Baptism and stanza 5 of Confirmation. The blessed Sacrament of Holy Communion is the theme of stanza 6, and the hymn closes with a song of praise to the Trinity, that note of doxology Franz-

mann so loved to raise. But more than that, this hymn is a summary of the liturgy of the church.

Another hymn which first appeared in the *Worship Supplement* was "O Kingly Love That Faithfully" (see p. 74). This hymn is found in the "Minor Festivals" section and is appointed for Reformation Day. The dominant image in the poem is that of God's love and of the "trumpet none could silence or mistake," the trumpet of God's Word played from His lips as a mighty blast "living and clear." Franzmann liked the trumpet image and used it in a number of places, but in the sermon titled "Ha! Ha! Among the Trumpets" the image is a strong forerunner of the hymn.

> *The* trumpet of God has sounded—one long, sonorous arabesque of sound which broke upon the midnight air when the angels brought good tidings of great joy to shepherds, and all the host of heaven made melody when the glory of the Lord shone 'round about them, a trumpet call that rose with a swell and a surge of sound as of the sound of many waters to rend the veil of the temple and to shake the earth to open all men's graves, when our Lord was crucified and rose again. And that trumpet call is for *us*: "This is the will of God in Christ Jesus concerning *you*." This trumpet call bids you snuff the Easter air, that air from which our Lord, upon the cross, has swept away all the dark poisonous vapors of sin, all the miasma of mortality; bids you scent that eternal air, and stamp that Easter-cloven ground, and to stand in triumph on your graves, and cry Ha! Ha!
>
> That blast reverberates through all the valleys of time and place, and all the trumpet calls that we shall hear in our ministry are but echoes and repercussions of that one triumphant blast. We shall hear the trumpets of God. We shall hear the cutting rigor of the stern and deep throated trumpet call to repentance: "Draw near to God, for He has drawn near to you! Turn ye, turn ye— from yourselves, and your sin, and your contorted revolt against your God. Repent for the kingdom of heaven has drawn near. And with it, at once, we shall hear the melody of mercy, the silver solace of the trumpet of forgiveness of our God, that trumpet which breathes the cross and tells us, "It is finished," and spells out for us with every silver tone, "Thy sins be forgiven thee." Greet that trumpet with resolute rejoicing. Say Ha! Ha! among these trumpets of God.

And with the sounding of these brave trumpets there is released also the eternal music, brave and resonant and pure, of love, that love which never faileth. It is the love of God that does not find but creates the object of its love—that love at work upon us, in us, and through us, to make our ministry a ministry like His who came to minister and give His life a ransom for many. Greet that trumpet call with a reckless selfgiving love that rejoices to spend and be spent, and thus your Ha! Ha! to that trumpet of God.[43]

The initial stanza personifies Love, meaning God, and points to His promises, promises kept by Him for the sake of His chosen people, His church. The next stanza focuses attention on the Sacrament of the Altar, that lavish banquet where "men might leave their puny care and taste and see how good Thou art." The third stanza makes reference to the parable of the king's banquet in Luke 14:16–24 where the invited guests refuse to come and the king sends his servant into the highways and byways so that his banquet hall might be filled. Here God's Love seeks with "hurrying feet" for "The bad and good on every street to fill Thy banquet hall."

Each of the first three stanzas is followed by a refrain of praise to God for raising up the mighty trumpet of His Word at the time of the Reformation, and throughout history, when man's foolish babble was drowning God's message of grace. The final stanza, which does not contain all of the refrain of the previous three stanzas, is a cry to God for mercy on mankind which has "drowned that song that once made every echo ring" with their "darkling cry" and "meddling sound" of contempt for the Lord and His Word of mercy and grace. It pleads with God to once again take up "the trumpet none can silence or mistake, And blow once more for all the world to hear, Living and clear:" that great message sent out by the king in Jesus' parable, God Himself: "The feast is ready—come to the feast, The Good and the bad, Come and be glad, Greatest and least, Come to the feast!"

"Weary of All Trumpeting" (see p. 76), written in 1971, first appeared in *Ecumenical Praise* (1972). It is another hymn in which Franzmann uses the image of the trumpet. At first the trumpet represents man's puny voice, with its message of unfulfilled promises, death, and destruction, which finally turns to God to plead for the heavenly song. In the second stanza the trumpet becomes the life-

giving Trumpet played by the breath of the Spirit, the message of the Gospel which calls us to follow Christ in His unselfish, dying love. The final stanza is a prayer to Christ to gather all people "To the triumph of Thy cross." The poet prays that God's people might come to a Christ-like life in which we "love by loss," gain "by giving," see in suffering the "triumph of surrender," and in dying "be partners in Thy splendor."

The 125th anniversary of The Lutheran Church—Missouri Synod was in 1972. Franzmann wrote the hymn "Thy Word Has Been Our Daily Bread" (see p. 77) to celebrate the occasion. It appeared in the July 2, 1972 edition of *The Lutheran Witness* under the simple title of "Anniversary Hymn." The theme of the hymn is the Word of God which the poet refers to no less than eight times in the first four stanzas of the six stanza hymn. An analysis of the hymn, stanza by stanza, reveals:

1. The Word is our "daily bread" both in its written form as well as in the person of Christ Jesus."

2. The Word is "eaten" by Christ's servants and binds us to our Lord.

3. The Word is God's clear and enduring promise to us.

4. This is a prayer for "the heart to heed Thy Word."

5. The Word now is taken and shared with others in order to bring in a harvest of souls.

6. Again Franzmann closes with a note of doxology.

Zion Lutheran Church in Dallas, Texas, celebrated the Rev. Carl A. Gaertner's 40th anniversary in the pastoral ministry on September 29, 1974. To aid in their celebration the congregation commissioned Martin Franzmann to write a hymn for the occasion and Donald Rotermund to provide the tune. Listed in the service folder under the heading "A Hymn for Called Servants of the Word" was the new hymn "O Thou, Who on Th' Accursed Ground (see p. 78)."[44]

A brief analysis of the hymn (stanza by stanza) follows:

1. God created the blessing of the Call in sin sick world of Old Testament times.

2. God chose Israel to be His people.

3. In a like manner Jesus called Matthew to be an apostle.

4/5. A song of thanksgiving for those called to the ministry.

6. The final stanza is a prayer.

Given Martin Franzmann's longtime and faithful service as a seminary teacher, it is fitting that we close with an ordination hymn by Franzmann, "Preach You the Word," (see p. 79), which was written for Concordia Seminary, Ft. Wayne and later appeared in the new hymnal of The Lutheran Church—Missouri Synod, *Lutheran Worship* (1982). (It also appears in *Christian Worship: A Lutheran Hymnal* (1993), published by the Wisconsin Evangelical Lutheran Synod, the church body of Franzmann's youth.) This is a hymn in which Professor Franzmann makes a final entreaty to those entering the Lord's ministry that they might preach God's word and "plant it home" whether or not others want to hear it, and whether or not they receive any rewards for their labors in this world. He then makes reference to the parable of the sower and the seed from Luke 8. The sower sows with a kind of reckless abandon and so do those who sow the seed of the Word. They sow that seed, they plant it home, they never faint because the Lord who gave the sower the seed in the first place "will watch and tend His planted Word."[45]

Notes

1 Martin H. Franzmann, *Ha! Ha! Among the Trumpets*, (St.Louis: Concordia Publishing House, 1966), 92.

2 *Ibid.*, p. 95.

3 *Ibid.*, pp. 96–97.

4 Martin H. Franzmann, "Christian Poetry," *Northwestern Lutheran* 33 (1946): 134.

5 *Ibid.*, p. 136.

6 *Ibid.*, p. 154.

7 *Ibid.*, p. 172.

8 *Ibid.*, p. 182.

9 *Ibid.*, p. 182.

10 Arthur F. Katt, *Critical Comments on the Proposed New Hymnal*, Shaker Heights, Ohio, July 15–September 15, 1939, p. 84.

11 *Ibid.*, p. 92.

12 *Ibid.*, p. 95.

13 *Ibid.*, p. 96.

14 W. G. Pollack, *The Handbook to the Lutheran Hymnal*, (St.Louis: Concordia Publishing House, 1958), 143.

15 Katt, *op. cit.*, pp. 88–89.

16 *Ibid.*, p. 89.

17 *Ibid.*, p. 89.

18 *Ibid.*, p. 90.

19 *Ibid.*, p. 86.

20 *Ibid.*, p. 86.

21 *Ibid.*, pp. 86–87.

22 *Ibid.*, p. 87.

23 *Ibid.*, p. 91.

24 *Ibid.*, p. 92.

25 *Ibid.*, p. 96.

26 *Ibid.*, p. 97.

27 F. R. Webber, "The Fine Arts in the Service of the Church," *American Lutheran* 20:6 (June 1937): 9.

28 Katt, *op. cit.*, pp. 99–100.

29 *Ibid.*, p. 100.

30 "Light from Above," *The Lutheran Witness* 73, no. 22 (October 26, 1954): 2.

31 Bruce R. Backer, *Lutheran Worship: A Course Guide* (New Ulm, Minnesota: Luther College, 1988), 129.

32 *Ibid.*, pp. 159–60.

33 Martin H. Franzmann, "Quick and Powerful," *Concordia Theological Monthly* 22, no. 3 (March 1951): 164, 168–69.

34 Martin H. Franzmann, "In Adam We Have All Been One," *A New Song* 680.

35 Martin H. Franzmann, "Augustana II: Of Original Sin," *Concordia Theological Monthly* 20:12 (December 1949): 885–86, 888–89.

36 Backer, *op. cit.*, pp. 129–30.

37 *Ibid.*, p. 160.

38 Martin H. Franzmann, "Christ, the Hope of Glory," *Concordia Theological Monthly* 24, no. 12 (December 1953): 900.

39 Martin H. Franzmann, "Reformation Hymn," manuscript dated September 23, 1966.

40 Backer, Bruce R., *op. cit.*, p. 160.

41 *Ibid.*, p. 159.

42 Werner Franzmann, interview, July 1992.

43 Martin H. Franzmann, "Ha! Ha! Among the Trumpets," *Ha! Ha! Among the Trumpets*, (St. Louis: Concordia Publishing House, 1966):4–5.

44 Service Folder, "A Service of Praise and Thanksgiving Celebrating the 40 Years in the Pastoral Ministry of The Reverend Carl A. Gaertner, D.D." Zion Lutheran Church, Dallas, Texas, September 29, 1974.

45 There may be three additional hymns as yet unpublished. The texts of these hymns, if they do indeed exist, were not available to this writer. These hymns are titled: "Lord Jesus Christ in Hidden Ways," "O First and Greatest of All Servants," and "You Spoke Your Word of Truth."

3

The Hymns and Translations in Recent Hymnals

A SURVEY OF ALTERATIONS MADE BY HYMNAL EDITORS

A number of Martin Franzmann's hymns have been included in recent hymnals, especially those produced within the Lutheran denominations. Several hymns have become popular with other church bodies as well. It is the purpose of this chapter to briefly examine the ways in which Franzmann's hymns have been employed in recent hymnals and to explore the changes made to those texts. (The new hymnal *Christian Worship: A Lutheran Hymnal,* published by the Wisconsin Evangelical Lutheran Synod, was not available for comparison when this book was written.)

The first of these hymns is "Thy Strong Word Did Cleave the Darkness" which appears in the following hymnals: *Worship Supplement* 747 (1969), *Worship II* 280 (1975), *Lutheran Book of Worship* 233 (1978), *Lutheran Worship* 328 (1982), *The Hymnal 1982* 381 (1985), *Rejoice in the Lord* 386 (1985), and *A New Hymnal* 9, 328 (1992). In every hymnal except one, this hymn is set to the melody *Ebenezer* (*Ton-y-botel*). The exception is *Rejoice in the Lord* which uses the tune *Lakeland.*

Most of the changes made in Franzmann's hymns could be termed "cosmetic" for they make little difference in the total scope of the hymn. They better represent current trends in language in recent years. One example is the use of lower case letters for pronouns referring to the Deity. Franzmann would always use an upper

case letter. He also preferred "Thee," "Thy," and "Thine" (now often considered archaic) over "You," "Your," and "Yours." The other change relates to gender bias. Franzmann retained forms of "man" when referring to humanity while many hymnals today opt for neutral words such as "those."

When the *Worship Supplement* was published in 1969, the editors made only slight changes in the capitalization of pronouns in "Thy Strong Word." *Worship II* uses the text as it appeared in the *Worship Supplement.* The editors of *Lutheran Book of Worship* followed the same pattern with the pronouns, they also made other changes. In the first line of stanza 2, the word "men" was replaced with "those" in an attempt to use "inclusive" language. In line four of the same stanza the word "life-breathing" was changed to "life-giving." The reason for this change would appear to be the fact that the line also contained "Breathed" and "breath." It might be argued that this minor alteration damages Franzmann's image of salvation in recalling God breathing into Adam the breath of life in Genesis 2:7. It also does harm to the alliteration created by the three words. In stanza 3, line 1 the editors capitalized "word," no doubt because of its obvious reference to Christ as the one who "bespeaks us righteous." The final stanza also contains some alterations to Franzmann's text and to his capitalization beyond pronouns. In line 1 "Light-Creator" becomes "light-creator," "Light-Revealer" is changed to "light-revealer" in line 5, "Men and angels, now and ever" becomes "Mortals, angels, now and ever" in line 7 and in the final line "Holy Trinity" becomes "holy Trinity." These changes were carried over to *Lutheran Worship* which retained the hymn in the same form as it appeared in *Lutheran Book of Worship.*

"Thy Strong Word" also appeared in *The Hymnal 1982* with the same alterations in the capitalization of pronouns and the same change in line 1 of stanza 2 "those" in place of "men." Here the editors included only stanzas 1 through 3 and 6. In stanza 6 they retained the capitalization of "Light-Creator," "Light-Revealer," and "Holy" as found in the *Worship Supplement.*

The most dramatic changes to "Thy Strong Word" occurred in *Rejoice in Lord* (1985). The editors chose the tune *Lakeland* for the hymn. However, the editors chose to combine stanzas, leaving out

large portions of Franzmann's original poem. The result, with dots placed to show where text has been left out, is given below.

1   Thy strong word did cleave the darkness;
At thy speaking it was done;
For created light we thank thee,
While Thy ordered seasons run.
    . . . .

On a world that dwelt in darkness,
Dark as night and deep as death,
Broke the light of thy salvation
Breathed thine own life giving breath.
    . . . .

2   Thy strong word bespeaks us righteous,
Bright with thine own holiness;
Glorious now, we press t'ward glory,
All our lives our hope confess.
    . . . .

From the cross thy wisdom shining
Breaketh forth in conqu'ring might;
From the cross forever beameth
All thy bright redeeming light.
    . . . .

Stanza 5 appears in its entirety so that the hymn closes with Franzmann's "alleluia" section, but the editors chose not to retain the doxological sixth stanza.

Several other changes were also made to Franzmann's text. Not content to change "men" to "these" at the beginning of Franzmann's second stanza (middle of stanza 1 above), the editors altered the words to read "On a world that dwelt in darkness." The word "Thine" in line 4 of the first stanza has been altered to "thy" and the word "hope" which appears in line 4 of stanza 1 above is a change from Franzmann's "hopes."

Another recent publication containing "Thy Strong Word" was *A New Hymnal* (1992). Here the text is the same as that found in *Worship II* with all of Franzmann's capitalization, other than pronouns, still intact and with "those" used in place of "men." The interesting thing about the use of the hymn in this hymnal is the fact that stanzas 1–5 appear together as hymn 9 in a section titled "In Praise of

God," while stanza 6, the doxological stanza, appears by itself as hymn 328 under the heading "Service Music."

"Weary of All Trumpeting" is another of Franzmann's hymns that has become very popular across denominational lines. It is found in the following hymnals: *Worship II* 310 (1975), *Ecumenical Praise* 113 (1977), *Hymnal 1982* 572 (1985), *United Methodist Hymnal* 442 (1989), and *A New Hymnal* 526 (1992). The only alteration made by the editors of any of these hymnals occurs in stanza 3 where, in the first and third lines, the word "men" is changed to "the" and to "we" respectively. These alterations are found in *The Hymnal 1982*, the *United Methodist Hymnal*, and *A New Hymnal* and are given below with the original text in parentheses.

> 3 To the triumph of your cross summon all the (men) living;
>   Summon us to love by loss, gaining all in giving,
>   Suffering all, that we (men) may see triumph in surrender;
>   Leaving all, that we (men) may be partners in your splendor.

"In Adam We Have All Been One" is a third hymn by Franzmann that has become quite popular. It appears in the following hymnals: *A New Song* 680 (1967), *Worship Supplement* 759 (1969), *Worship II* 136 (1975), *Lutheran Book of Worship* 372 (1978), and *Lutheran Worship* 292 (1982). This hymn also appeared in *More Hymns for Today*, a British publication which was not available for comparison.

A New Song contains the text with Franzmann's capitalization of pronouns referring to God, but the *Worship Supplement* removes the capital letters while retaining the rest of the text intact. *Worship II* retains the text as it is found in the *Worship Supplement* with one small change. The word "Shepherd" as found in line 3 of stanza 3 is no longer capitalized. This was no doubt done since the word preceding "shepherd" is the word "his" which is also not capitalized. *Lutheran Book of Worship* retains all the changes made in *Worship II* with the words "Evening Voice" in line 3 of stanza 1 written "evening voice." This change removes some of Franzmann's emphasis on the "Voice" being God Himself, although the context makes it clear enough. One other small change occurs in line 2 of stanza

5 where the poetic "O" is replaced by "Oh." *Lutheran Worship* retains the changes already noted, and it also contains some of the most significant deviations from Franzmann's original. First, the editors dropped "Thee" and "Thou" and replaced them with "you" and "your." Then they made some major changes in the text itself. In stanza 2, line 1 which Franzmann wrote as "We fled Thee, and in losing Thee" became "We fled our God, and, fleeing him." Stanza 4, line 2 was changed from "Didst love and save us all" to "You loved and saved us all." Also, in stanza 4, line 3 the words "Good Shepherd" are given "good shepherd" even though the reference is clearly to Christ. Stanza 6, line 4 has one minor change beyond the substitution of "you" for "Thou." It is the use of the word "are" in place of "art."

The largest revision of the text occurs in stanza 5. Below is given Franzmann's original of stanza 5 side by side with the revision.

Altered	*Original*
Send us *your* Spirit, teach us truth;	Send us Thy Spirit, teach us truth;
To purge our vanity;	Thou Son, O set us free
From fancied wisdom, self-sought ways,	From fancied wisdom, self-sought ways,
O Savior, set us free.	To make us one in Thee.

While the alteration does not radically change Franzmann's meaning, the resulting redundancy seems unnecessary. It is a reminder of what Arthur Katt said back in 1939 about people placing "unholy hands" on the texts of our hymns.[1] (See pp. 56–57 for the entire quote.)

"O God, O Lord of Heaven and Earth," which was written for the 450th anniversary of the Reformation in 1967, appears in the following hymnals: *Worship Supplement* 759 (1969), *Worship II* 199 (1975), *Lutheran Book of Worship* 396 (1978), and *Lutheran Worship* 319 (1982).

Both the *Worship Supplement* and *Worship II* retain the same minor changes. In stanza 2, line 7 the words "Prince of Peace" are given as "Prince of peace" and in stanza 4, line 4 the word "church" as it is found in the manuscript dated September 1966, is written "Church."

THY STRONG WORD

The two recent Lutheran Hymnals, *Lutheran Book of Worship* and *Lutheran Worship*, contain a number of significant alterations. The two hymnals present the text in an identical fashion. The altered text is given below with the text as found in the manuscript. Differences in the altered text are in italic

Altered	*Original*
1 O God, O Lord of heaven and earth,	O God, O Lord of heaven and earth,
Your living finger never wrote	Thy living finger never wrote
That life should be an aimless mote,	That life should be an aimless mote,
A deathward drift from futile birth.	A deathward drift from futile birth.
Your Word meant life triumphant hurled	Thy Word meant life triumphant hurled
In splendor through your broken world;	Through every cranny of Thy world.
Since light awoke and life began,	Since light awoke and life began,
You made for us a holy plan.	Thou hast desired Thy life for man.
2 *In blind revolt we would not see*	Our fatal will to equal Thee,
That rebel *wills* wrought death and night.	Our rebel will wrought death and night.
We seized and used in *fear and spite*	We seized and used in Thy despite
Your wondrous gift of liberty.	Thy wondrous gift of liberty.
We *walled* us in this house of doom,	We housed us in this house of doom,
Where death had royal scope and room,	Where death had royal scope and room,
Until *your* servant, Prince, of Peace,	Until Thy servant, Prince of Peace,
Broke down its walls for our release.	Breached all its walls for our release.
3 *You came* into our hall of death,	Thou camest to our hall of death,

O Christ, to breathe our poisoned air,	O Christ, to breathe our poisoned air,
To drink for us the *deep* despair	To drink for us the dark despair
That strangled *our* reluctant breath.	That strangled man's reluctant breath.
How beautiful the feet that trod	How beautiful the feet that trod
The road *to bring good news from God!*	The road that leads us back to God!
How beautiful the feet that *bring*	How beautiful the feet that ran
Good tidings of our saving king!	To bring the great good news to man!

4	O Spirit who *did* once restore	O Spirit, who didst once restore
	The Church, that it *might once recall*	Thy Church that it may be again
	The bringer of good news to *all:*	The bringer of good news to men,
	Breathe on *your* cloven church once more,	Breathe on Thy cloven church once more,
	That in these gray and latter days	That in these gray and latter days
	There may be *those* whose life is praise,	There may be men whose life is praise,
	Each life a high doxology	Each life a high doxology
	Unto the holy Trinity.	To Father, Son, and unto Thee.

Some of the changes appear to be an attempt to make what Bruce Backer thought were difficulties created when a "student of the classics writes hymns" more acceptable.[2] (See p. 88.) The changes in the second stanza would seem to be this sort of "correction." The most significant alteration is the shift of sense that is created by the changes in stanza 3. In Franzmann's original it is Christ who charts the road back to God for us and runs to us with the Good News. The hymn is altered so that the direction in both cases is from God to man. Through this alteration we lose the sense of Christ going on before us. The changes in stanza 4 also create a shift in sense. In the original it is the church which, through the

power of the Spirit, is the bringer of good news, but in the altered version the church merely recalls while the Spirit becomes the active vehicle. The meaning is fundamentally the same, but Franzmann's is more poetic.

Franzmann's setting of the Lord's Prayer, "O Thou, Who Hast of Thy Pure Grace," was published in both the *Worship Supplement* 767 (1969) and *Lutheran Book of Worship* 442 (1978). The texts are identical with the only change from the original being the capitalization of the pronouns.

The hymn "O Kingly Love, That Faithfully" can be found in the *Worship Supplement* 757 (1969) and in *Lutheran Worship* 346 (1982). The texts are exactly alike and have no alterations other than to the capitalization of the pronouns. (See pp. 74–75 for Franzmann's text.)

"O Fearful Place, Where He Who Knows Our Heart" was written to celebrate a church anniversary. It has appeared only in the *Worship Supplement* 774 (1969). It can be assumed that the pronouns in Franzmann's original would have been capitalized for that is consistent with his practice and style. (See p. 73 for the text.)

"Preach You the Word" is found only in official books—*Lutheran Worship* 259 (1982) and in *Christian Worship: A Lutheran Hymnal* 554 (1993). It is difficult to tell without a copy of the manuscript whether Franzmann used the pronouns "you" and "your" in reference to God or if those words were minor alterations made by the editors.

Three of Franzmann's translations have appeared in modern hymnals. The first dates back to 1934 and is titled "Rise Again, Ye Lion-Hearted" which appeared in *The Lutheran Hymnal* 470 (1941). The editors made only one small change from the original. This change is found in the final line of the last stanza. The original reads "Grant that I may ever be, Loyal knight and true to Thee!" This was altered to read "Grant that I may ever be, Loyal, staunch, and true to Thee!"

The second translation also dates from 1934 and is the version of Luther's "Jesaia, dem Propheten" which Katt so fervently wanted included in *The Lutheran Hymnal*. (See pp. 53–54 and 44.) It took nearly 40 years, but, in 1978, *Lutheran Book of Worship* used Franz-

mann's translation with only one very small change. The archaic word "twain" was replaced with "two."

The final translation used in recent hymnals is "With High Delight Let Us Unite" which can be found in the *Worship Supplement* 734 (1969), *Lutheran Book of Worship* 140 (1978), and *Lutheran Worship* 134 (1982). (See p. 52 for the text.) A comparison of the *Worship Supplement* and *Lutheran Worship* shows the only changes from the original, other than pronoun capitalization, to be:

1. The second line of the first stanza, "In songs of great jubilation" was changed to "In songs of sweet jubilation."
2. "His enemy vanquished doth lie" in stanza 2, line 3, was altered to read "His enemy shall vanquished lie."
3. The word "saith" in line 6 of stanza 2 was changed to "said."
4. The words "Jesus Christ, our Salvation" were changed to "Jesus Christ, our salvation."
5. The replacement of "ye" with "you."

An examination of the text found in *Lutheran Book of Worship* reveals several more substantial changes beyond those found in *Lutheran Worship* and the *Worship Supplement.* Yet these changes do not alter Franzmann's meaning:

1. Stanza 1, line 3, which read "You pure in heart, all bear your part" was changed to "You pure in heart, each take your part."
2. The other change occurred in line 3 of stanza 2 where, like in *Lutheran Book of Worship*, "His enemy vanquished doth lie" was altered to read "His enemy shall vanquished lie."

Of Franzmann's translations and original hymns a number have yet to be included in any hymnbook. The translation list:

> "Christ, Our Lord, Arose" (see p. 45)
> "The Dawn Has Driven Dark Night Away" (see pp. 46–47)
> "Jesus, Only, Naught But Jesus" (see p. 48)
> "Praise Thou the Lord, My Soul, Praise and Adore Him" (see p. 49)
> "O Lord, We Praise Thee" (see p. 50)

"To Songs of Joy Awake Thee" (see p. 51)
Original Hymns:
"Though Wisdom All Her Skills Combine" (see p. 65)
"O Thou Whose Fiery Blessing Can" (see p. 68)
"Our Lord Has Laid His Benison" (see p. 71)
"O Thou, Who on Th' Accursed Ground" (see p. 78)
"Thy Word Has Been Our Daily Bread" (see p. 77)

It can be fairly said that, for the most part, the editors of hymnals have been kind to Franzmann's original words and meaning. However, we have seen that several hymns have undergone some substantial changes. There are also a significant number of Franzmann's hymns that have not been published to any great extent. It remains for editors of future hymnals, and for composers of music for the church, to make good use of the legacy of fine poetry which Martin Franzmann has bequeathed to the church.

Notes

1 Arthur Katt, *Critical Comments on the Proposed New Hymnal,* Shaker Heights, Ohio, July 15–September 15, 1939, p. 86.
2 Bruce R. Backer, *Lutheran Worship: A Course Guide,* 4th ed. (New Ulm, Minnesota: Luther College, 1988), 159.

4

The Hymns and Translations: Some Conclusions

WHAT MAKES FOR A FINE HYMN? AN APPRAISAL OF FRANZMANN'S WORK

What is it that makes a hymn or translation "good"? Is it the quality of the poetry alone: rhythm, rhyme, meter, and imagery? Is it the faith of the writer that comes through in the text of the hymn? Is it a solid biblical content in the hymn? Does the hymn have to make an application to those who read or sing it? Is it the use of imagery to which the "common person" can relate? Does the hymn text have to move the emotions? Or is that the responsibility of the melody? What makes for a "good" hymn, and what in Franzmann's hymns makes them outstanding?

Bruce R. Backer of Dr. Martin Luther College, New Ulm, Minnesota, gives us some insights and a basis on which to evaluate and attempt to answer the question given above. For Backer there are nine areas that a "good" hymn addresses. They are as follows:

1. *A good hymn is liturgical.* This type of hymn makes an address to God or it calls others to do so.

2. *A good hymn is doxological.* A good doxology does more than "Praise the Lord"; it attributes to Him names and tells what He does for His people through each person of the Godhead.

3. *A good hymn has doctrinal content.* That is, the hymn teaches about God and His activity on behalf of humanity, especially in His act of redemption through Christ Jesus.

4. *A good hymn makes use of the word of God.* Here the hymn quotes the Scriptures. It uses stories or images taken from the Bible to strengthen its message.

5. *A good hymn applies the message.* The content of the hymn is applied to the daily lives of God's people today.

6. *A good hymn is poetry with choice of words, thought progressions, and word pictures that are drawn from experiences common to many people.* Simple words, thoughts, word pictures, and images common to the experience of our day are what is meant here.

7. *A good hymn has an emotional component that supports the message.* The emotion grows *from* the message and reinforces it.

8. *A good hymn is influenced by the church year.* Good hymns speak of the events in the life of Christ that are of such great importance to His people. His birth, death, resurrection, and ascension are retold and are applied to our lives today.

9. *Good hymns have melodies that bear the accent of eternity and touch the heart of the worshiper.* The sights and sounds that the worshiper encounters in church must be those that point to the "other worldliness" of the faith, that we are but strangers and pilgrims in a foreign land, that heaven is our true home.[1]

How do Martin Franzmann's hymns stand up to these criteria? The balance of this chapter will explore this question and will attempt to show that Franzmann's hymns represent the best in the hymnwriter's art.

Liturgical Expression

Martin Franzmann was a master of the art of liturgical expression. The following excerpts from his hymns demonstrate his address of the Persons of the Trinity. First, how does he address the Father?

THY STRONG WORD DID CLEAVE THE DARKNESS
(STANZA 1)

Thy strong word did cleave the darkness;
At Thy speaking it was done.
For created light we thank Thee,
While Thine ordered seasons run. . . .

O GOD, O LORD OF HEAV'N AND EARTH
(STANZA 1)

O God, O Lord of heav'n and earth
Your living finger never wrote
That life should be an aimless mote,
A deathward drift from futile birth. . . .

IN ADAM WE HAVE ALL BEEN ONE
(STANZA 2)

We fled Thee, and in losing Thee
We lost our brother too;
Each singly sought and claimed his own;
Each man his brother slew.

PRAISE THOU THE LORD, MY SOUL, PRAISE AND ADORE HIM
(TRANSLATION, STANZA 1)

Praise Thou the Lord, my soul, praise and adore Him,
While pulse and breath and being last:
Ever with laud and praise coming before Him,
I'll sing my God till life be past. . . .

THE DAWN HAS DRIVEN DARK NIGHT AWAY
(TRANSLATION, STANZA 11)

Pray thou the Father: "Thanks to Thee,
That art from all eternity,
For Thy bounteous blessings,"

THY STRONG WORD

The following excerpts address God the Son.

O Lord, We Praise Thee, Bless Thee, and Adore Thee
(Translation)

O Lord, we praise Thee, bless Thee, and adore Thee,
Giving thanks, we bow before Thee,
That with Thy blood and body Thou hast fed us,
May Thy gift, Lord, well bestead us! . . .

With High Delight Let Us Unite
(Translation, Stanza 3)

Let praises ring; give thanks, and bring
To Christ our Lord adoration.
His honor spread by word and deed
To every land and nation. . . .

In Adam We Have All Been One
(Stanza 4)

O Thou who, when we loved Thee not,
Didst love and save us all,
Thou great Good Shepherd of mankind,
O hear us when we call.

O God, O Lord of Heaven and Earth
(Stanza 3)

Thou camest to our hall of death,
O Christ, to breathe our poisoned air,
To drink for us the dark despair
That strangled man's reluctant breath.
How beautiful the feet that trod
The road which leads us back to God!
How beautiful the feet that ran
To bring the great good news to man!

JESUS ONLY, NAUGHT BUT JESUS
(TRANSLATION, STANZA 5)

Lord, with many another blessing
    Thou hast given Thyself to me:
Let me then with praise unceasing
    Sing the burden joyfully:
Thou my life dost guard and shield,
Lead me, Lord, e'en as Thou wilt!

THE DAWN HAS DRIVEN DARK NIGHT AWAY
(TRANSLATION, STANZAS 12–13)

Through Jesus Christ, unto Whose praise,
As unto Thee, the angels raise
Voice and song in heaven.

And as they praise Thee, Lord, may I
Henceforth to all eternity
Ever praise Thee. Amen.

And, finally, these stanzas are examples of address to God the Holy Spirit.

THOU WISDOM ALL HER SKILLS COMBINE
(STANZA 5)

The Comforter be praised, Whom He,
Th' ascended God, to us hath sent. . . .

THY STRONG WORD DID CLEAVE THE DARKNESS
(STANZA 6)

Holy Spirit, Light-Revealer,
Glory, glory be to Thee.

O GOD, O LORD OF HEAVEN AND EARTH
(STANZA 4)

O Spirit, who didst once restore
Thy Church that it may be again
The bringer of good news to men,
Breathe on Thy cloven church once more . . . .

Doxology

The doxology has already been noted as one of Franzmann's favorite means of expression. Not only are doxologies found in abundance in his hymns, but his writings also abound with them. (See quote on p. 35.)

THOU WISDOM ALL HER SKILLS COMBINE
(STANZA 5)

Then praise to God the Father be,
His Saviour Son to us Who lent:
The Comforter be Praised, Whom He,
Th' ascended God, to us hath sent:
    And praise to Thee, O Christ, true God,
    Though in our ways Thy feet have trod.

IN ADAM WE HAVE ALL BEEN ONE
(STANZA 6)

Then shall our song united rise
To Thine eternal throne,
Where with the Father evermore
And Spirit Thou art One.

O FEARFUL PLACE, WHERE HE WHO KNOWS OUR HEART
(STANZA 7)

O God Almighty, gracious Three in One,
In this Thy house let praises to Thee be done
Until we join in heaven's high unison:
Alleluia! Alleluia!

OUR LORD HAS LAID HIS BENISON
(STANZA 8)

To God our Father through the Son
All glory, laud, and honor be,
And to the Spirit, with Them One,
Now and eternally.

THY STRONG WORD DID CLEAVE THE DARKNESS (STANZA 6)

God the Father, Light-Creator,
To Thee laud and honor be;
To Thee, Light of Light begotten,
Praise be sung eternally;
Holy Spirit, Light-Revealer,
Glory, glory be to Thee;
Men and angels, now and ever
Praise the Holy Trinity.

This last doxology has been called by Bruce Backer the greatest doxology ever penned, not only in the English language, but "in the entire corpus of western hymnody."[2]

Doctrinal Expression

The hymns of Franzmann are also rich with doctrinal expression. His hymn "In Adam We Have All Been One" clearly presents the doctrine of original sin in all its truth. "This doctrine has been openly denied by some, outwardly accepted but inwardly denied by others, but confessed with great joy by the believing Church."[3]

In Adam we have all been one,
One huge rebellious man;
We all have fled that Evening Voice
That sought us as we ran.

We fled Thee, and in losing Thee
We lost our brother too;
Each singly sought and claimed his own,
Each man his brother slew.

Stanza 2 of "O God, O Lord of Heaven and Earth" also clearly proclaims the doctrine of original sin.

Our fatal will to equal Thee,
Our rebel will wrought death and night.
We seized and used in Thy despite
Thy wondrous gift of liberty.
We housed us in this house of doom,
Where death had royal scope and room,
Until Thy Servant, Prince of Peace,
Breached all its walls for our release.

110

A hymn that deals with the deity of Christ is "Thou Art the Christ, the Son of the Living God" (see p. 65). Franzmann uses a refrain that, as Katt rightly noted, drives home, deep into a person, that Jesus is the Son of God.[4] The entire hymn points to Christ's divinity. Stanza 1 reminds the reader that Jesus is "from everlasting to everlasting." Stanza 2 proclaims the mystery of God incarnate. Stanza 3 points to the cross, to the awful sacrifice of the Son of God for a sin-sick world. The triumph of the resurrection is declared in stanza 4, and stanza 5 speaks of His ascension to the right hand of glory in heaven. Through the entire hymn the refrain sounds again and again until it reaches the worshiper's soul:

> Thou art the Christ, Thou art the God,
> Though in our ways Thy feet have trod!

In the last stanza the deity of Christ is stated in even stronger terms.

> And praise to Thee, O Christ, true God,
> Though in our ways Thy feet have trod.

The doctrine of the church is the theme of "O Fearful Place, Where He Who Knows Our Heart" (see p. 73). The role of Christ's church in the lives of His redeemed children is proclaimed stanza after stanza. Here in the seven stanzas of this hymn, we find: the proclamation of the Law that convicts us of our sin, the presence of God among His people, the announcement of the Absolution, Baptism, Confirmation, and the Lord's Supper.

The doctrine of the Real Presence in the Sacrament of the Altar is the theme of Franzmann's excellent translation of the first stanza of the German hymn "Gott sei gelobet."

O LORD, WE PRAISE THEE, BLESS THEE AND ADORE THEE

> Giving thanks we bow before Thee,
>   That with Thy blood and body Thou hast fed us,
> May this gift, Lord, well bestead us!
>   Kyrie Eleison!
> O Thou virgin-born, our Savior Lord,
> By Thy body broken, Thy blood outpoured,
>   As in life, so in death
>   Be Thou He that succoureth!
>   Kyrie Eleison!

111

The hymns of Martin Franzmann are filled with examples of clear doctrinal expression. The few stanzas cited here are but a small sampling of Franzmann's skill in this area. A careful study of all his hymn texts will disclose many others to one who studies and sings them.

Use of the Word of God

The clearest example of the use of the word of God in hymns would be all the various hymns that are a recasting of one or another of the psalms. Another way the word of God can be used is by making a scriptural quote in a hymn. A third technique is to refer to a Biblical story. It is in the use of biblical images and stories that Franzmann is a master.

In the hymn "O Fearful Place, Where He Who Knows Our Heart" the image of Jacob's dream (Genesis 28:16), where he saw heaven opened and the angels of God ascending and descending, is clearly presented in the second and third stanzas.

> O House of God, where angel troops descend
> From heaven to man and on His saints attend;
> Here let us sing the song that knows no end:
>   Alleluia! Alleluia!
> O gate of heaven, where God's almighty Word,
> Big with forgiveness, constantly is heard,
> And God's elect to shouts of praise are stirred:
>   Alleluia! Alleluia!

The parable of the sower and the seed from Luke 8 forms the basis for the hymn "Preach You the Word and Plant It Home." The second and third stanzas are given here to show how Franzmann uses this story, told by Jesus, to make a point about the role of God's servants in His ministry.

> The sower sows; his reckless love
>   Scatters abroad the goodly seed,
> Intent alone that men may have
>   The wholesome loaves that all men need.
> Though some be snatched and some be scorched
>   And some be choked and matted flat,
> The sower sows; his heart cries out,
>   "Oh, what of that, and what of that?"

Four separate biblical images are found in "Our Lord Has Laid His Benison." The first is the wedding feast at Cana recorded in John 2.

> No stranger to the wedding feast,
> At Cana, when the wine was spent,
> He largely gave, and gave the best,
> For family merriment.

In Mark 10:14–15 Jesus rebukes those who would forbid the mothers to bring their small children to Him and uses the children to point out the kind of faith one must have as one of His disciples. Franzmann makes use of this event to point out the same truth that Jesus did, that we are all, young and old alike, His children.

> He bade the timid mothers bring
> Their children to Him to be blessed,
> And promised that for such the King
> Is King above the rest.

In the fourth stanza of this hymn Franzmann makes use of the story of the death of Lazarus (John 11:1–44) to show us the compassion of Jesus for our families even in their hour of greatest grief.

> He lived with us, He wept with us,
> He knew our human pangs and fears
> When Mary wept for Lazarus,
> He did not stay His tears.

The call of St. Matthew (Mark 2:14) from his work as a tax collector to that of a disciple is found in the third stanza of "O Thou, Who on the Accursed Ground."

> O Thou, who from his grubby wealth
> Didst once Thy servant Matthew call,
> To leave that rubbish for Thy gold
> To speak Thy word to nations all.

In Isaiah 6 the prophet sees the glory of God and fears his life is ended, but the angel of God (a seraphim) takes a burning coal and touches Isaiah's lips declaring him clean and righteous before God. The power of God's word to make righteous people out of men who have unclean lips is the theme of "O Thou, Whose Fiery Blessing." In the first stanza Franzmann draws on this event in the life of Isaiah.

O Thou, whose fiery blessing can
Make pure the unclean lips of man;
That takest man and makest him
A singer with the seraphim;

The children who sang Jesus' praises (Matthew 21:15) that first
Palm Sunday as He entered Jerusalem seated on a donkey's back
are reflected in the second stanza of this same hymn.

O Thou that buildest mighty praise
From shouts that children's voices raise;
That canst when human voices die,
Make silent stones to prophesy:

Application of the Message

Franzmann applies Adam and Eve's rebellion to us today in
stanza 5 of "In Adam We Have All Been One." We need to hear
and know God's truth, not our "fancied wisdom" or our "self-sought
ways."

Send us Thy Spirit, teach us truth;
Thou Son, O set us free
From fancied wisdom, self-sought ways,
To make us one in Thee.

The Light that comes from above, the Wisdom of God come
down in human form, Who leads captive humanity free, is the
theme of "Thy Strong Word Did Cleave the Darkness." The application comes in stanza 5, which tells us that we are to praise this
marvelous God who gives us His blessed Light. This is the Light that
shines "out of darkness, to give the light of the glory of God in the
face of Jesus Christ" (2 Corinthians 4:6).

Give us lips to sing Thy glory,
Tongues Thy mercy to proclaim,
Throats that shout the hope that fills us,
Mouths to speak Thy holy name . . .

The closing lines of the refrain in "O Kingly Love, That Faithfully" make application to the worshipers. God has prepared His
banquet hall and all who love His coming are invited, not because
of their merits, but wholly because He loves them.

> The feast is ready—come to the feast,
> The good and the bad,
> Come and be glad,
> Greatest and least,
> Come to the feast.

A strong image of discipleship is projected in the hymn "Weary of All Trumpeting." Here Franzmann lays out for us the Christ-like life, one of service not of self.

> To the triumph of your cross summon all men living;
> Summon us to love by loss, gaining all by giving,
> Suffering all, that men may see triumph in surrender;
> Leaving all, that we may be partners in your splendor.

The example of Jesus' love and caring within the context of family life is the theme of "Our Lord Has Laid His Benison." After showing us examples of Jesus' giving love in stanzas 1–6, Franzmann then applies it all to our family lives.

> Let all our ties of heart and mind
> By Thy great love transfigured be,
> And may these bonds be bonds that bind
> Us each to each and Thee!

The hymn Franzmann wrote for the 125th anniversary of the founding of The Lutheran Church — Missouri Synod was titled "Thy Word Had Been Our Daily Bread." Here he focuses our attention on the Word and its power to transform and sustain Christ's church on earth. The application comes in stanza 4 where Franzmann writes:

> Grant us the heart to heed Thy Word,
> Give us the strength to be
> Thy friends who serve, not duty bound,
> But free as Thou art free.

A Good Hymn Is Good Poetry

Good hymns are poems that are able to take the language of poetry and use it so that the message is communicated in words that rise above simple prose. Yet they are not so encumbered with "art" that the common person is unable to grasp the poem's width and depth and height. The hymnwriter walks a ground that lies

between simple rhyming prose and exalted language. The truly great hymns are those that go beyond the mere formalities of poetry to lift our hearts to a greater level of understanding and emotion regarding the Christian faith. Such hymns enable us to grasp the great truths of God's Word with a deeper comprehension than prose could ever express. Many of Franzmann's hymns and translations take us to that region of exalted praise.

Observe how, in his translation of Herrnschmidt's "Lobe den Herren, o meine Seele," Franzmann sweeps us into the praise of the saints before God's throne.

> Praise thou the Lord, my soul, praise and adore Him,
> While pulse and breath and being last:
> Ever with laud and praise coming before Him,
> I'll sing my God till life be past:
> Thou God who hast created me
> Both soon and late shalt praised be!
> Alleluia! Alleluia!

"Thy Strong Word Did Cleave the Darkness" is another fine example of Franzmann's ability with poetic language. This hymn has become one of the most widely known and used of his hymns. His treatment of God's redemption of humanity expresses at once the tremendous power of God's hand and His great love for us. Stanzas 2 and 3 are quoted below.

> Lo, on men who dwelt in darkness,
> Dark as night and deep as death,
> Broke the light of Thy salvation,
> Breathed Thine own life-breathing breath:
> Alleluia! Alleluia!
> Praise to Thee who light dost send!
> Alleluia! Alleluia!
> Alleluia without end!
>
> Thy strong word bespeaks us righteous;
> Bright with Thine own holiness,
> Glorious now, we press toward glory,
> And our lives our hopes confess:
> Alleluia! Alleluia!
> Praise to Thee who light dost send!
> Alleluia! Alleluia!
> Alleluia without end!

Franzmann was also capable of writing hymns that contained more difficult words and ideas. Some have criticized him as being, at times, too difficult owing to his background as a scholar and university professor.[5] Yet, with a little effort, even a hymn such as "O God, O Lord of Heaven and Earth" is not beyond the grasp of most people. The quality of the hymn overshadows any minor difficulties created by his choice of words and images. Note how stanza 1 "sings."

> O God, O Lord of heaven and earth,
> Thy living finger never wrote
> That life should be an aimless mote,
> A deathward drift from futile birth.
> Thy Word meant life triumphant hurled
> Through every cranny of our world.
> Since light awoke and life began,
> Thou hast desired Thy life for man.

Possibly Franzmann's finest poetry is found in the hymn "O Kingly Love, That Faithfully." The entire hymn, but especially the final stanza, is profoundly and powerfully moving verse.

> O holy Love, Thou canst not brook
> Man's cool and careless enmity;
> O ruthless Love, Thou wilt not look
> On man robed in contempt of Thee.
>> Thine echoes die;
>> Our deeds deny
>> Thy summoning:
>> Our darkling cry,
>> Our meddling sound
>> Have all but drowned
>> That song that made every echo ring.
> Take up again, O take
> The trumpet none could silence or mistake
> And blow once more for all the world to hear,
> Living and clear:
>> The feast is ready, come to the feast,
>> The good and the bad,
>> Come and be glad,
>> Greatest and least,
>> Come to the feast!

The Emotional Component

Joy is a powerful and all-encompassing emotion. It can arise from great happiness and also from profound grief. The joy of the Scriptures is not dependent on the circumstances of earthly life. St. Paul well understood this when he said, "Rejoice in the Lord always. I will say it again: Rejoice!" (Phillipians 4:4).[6] He knew how to abound in joy in all situations of life. Joy is the message of salvation; God is with us, He has come and redeemed His people. Franzmann's hymns speak of and to this kind of joy.

Franzmann's translation of "Jesus, Jesus, nichts als Jesus" talks of this kind of joy that can arise in any and all situations in life. Here he writes:

> Lord, with many another blessing
> Thou hast given Thyself to me:
> Let me then with praise unceasing
> Sing the burden joyfully:
> Thou my life dost guard and shield,
> Lead me, Lord, e'en as Thou wilt!

The same joy is spoken of in stanza 3 of his translation "With High Delight Let Us Unite."

> Let praises ring; give thanks, and bring
> To Christ our Lord adoration.
> His honor spread by word and deed
> To every land, every nation.
> So shall His love give us above,
> From misery and death set free,
> All joy and full consolation.

In his first hymn, "Though Wisdom All Her Skills Combine," Franzmann writes of this joy in the second stanza:

> I joy to own the mystery
> That veils Thy birth from human ken:
> Thy godhead there I chiefly see,
> Where love hath made Thee Man of men:
>> Thou art the Christ, Thou art the God,
>> Though in our ways Thy feet have trod.

The struggle and the joy of the Christian life are presented in stanza 3 of "Weary of All Trumpeting."

118

To the triumph of your cross summon all men living;
Summon us to love by loss, gaining all by giving,
Suffering all, that men may see triumph in surrender;
Leaving all, that we may be partners in your splendor.

Good Hymn Writing and the Church Year

Good hymns bring to our remembrance the events of the life of Christ. They follow the cycle of the church year with its seasons focused on the principal events in the story of salvation through Jesus Christ. While only a few of the hymns and translations are truly "seasonal hymns," Franzmann's hymns do have sprinkled throughout them the events of the Savior's life: the promise of a Savior; His birth; His life; His death on the cross of Calvary; and His resurrection and ascension.

Isaiah 9:2 speaks of the promised Savior as a light shining in darkness when Isaiah says: "The people walking in darkness have seen a great light; on those living in the land of the shadow of death a light has dawned."[7] Franzmann picks up on this Advent image from Isaiah in stanza 2 of "Thy Strong Word Did Cleave the Darkness."

Lo, on men who dwelt in darkness,
Dark as night and deep as death,
Broke the light of Thy salvation,
Breathed Thine own life-breathing breath:

Franzmann writes of the incarnation and birth of the Savior in stanza 2 of "Thou Wisdom All Her Skills Combine."

I joy to own the mystery
That veils Thy birth from human ken;
Thy godhead there I chiefly see,
Where love hath made Thee Man of men:

Many of the events from Jesus ministry are alluded to by Franzmann in his hymns. The hymn "Our Lord Has Laid His Benison" devotes four stanzas (2–5) to various moments in the Lord's earthly ministry.

The death of Jesus is mentioned in many places in Franzmann's hymns. The following stanza (4) taken from "Thy Strong Word Did Cleave the Darkness" serves as an example.

> From the cross Thy wisdom shining
> Breaketh forth in conquering might;
> From the cross forever beameth
> All Thy bright redeeming light:

The resurrection is also referred to in many of the hymns and translations. Two translations "Christ, Our Lord, Arose" and "To Songs of Joy Awake Thee" respectively are seasonal hymns which deal with the resurrection. (see pp. 45 and 51) An example from the hymns is found in stanza 6 of "Our Lord Has Laid His Benison."

> O Thou, who once in Thy sole death
> Hast borne and buried all our sin
> And by Thy life hast given breath
> To all Thy ransomed kin,

Melodies That Support and Enhance

The final area in the discussion of qualities that make up a good hymn is that of melody. Melodies do have something to say if they are well crafted. Franzmann wrote his hymns, in many cases, with a particular melody in mind. When given the opportunity he would suggest tunes to be used with his hymns. A number of the hymns appeared in the *Lutheran Witness* with notes concerning the tunes to which they should be sung. The tunes used with Franzmann's hymns do, in most cases, support and enhance the meaning of the hymn.

The tune *Ebenezer*, which is used with "Thy Strong Word Did Cleave the Darkness," is a perfect example of this wedding of tune and text. The rock-solid rhythm and rugged melody of this tune are a perfect match to the powerful words of Franzmann's hymn.

Richard Hillert composed the melody *Kingly Love*, which is used with "O Kingly Love, That Faithfully." Here again the melody is perfectly attuned to the text. The repeated notes that occur throughout the melody remind us of the trumpet image that Franzmann uses in this hymn.

It is not necessary that every hymn satisfy every criterion. A good hymn will express a number of these qualities but not necessarily all of them. Based on the criteria established at the beginning of this chapter, it is clear that the hymns of Martin Franzmann are

of the highest quality. The excellence of his work cannot be denied, but the real test is that of time. It remains for the future to tell for sure if these hymns are in the group that endures through the ages.

Martin Franzmann was, throughout his life, a teacher. Those who knew him personally knew that in his presence all were his students. As one writer said, "All who ever sat at Dr. Franzmann's feet—and who of his myriad acquaintances cannot be said to have sat at his feet whenever in his presence?—will remember always the depth of his knowledge and understanding of the scriptures."[8] This quality of "teacher" lives on in his writings and especially in his hymns. Anyone who spends time with these hymns—reads them, sings them, ponders them—will sit at Martin Franzmann's feet and learn from him.

Notes

1   Bruce R. Backer, *Lutheran Worship: A Course Guide,* 4th ed. (New Ulm, Minnesota: Luther College, 1988), 125ff.

2   *Ibid.*, p. 129.

3   *Ibid.*, p. 129.

4   Arthur F.Katt, *Critical Comments on the Proposed New Hymnal*, Shaker Heights, Ohio, July 15–September 15, 1939, p. 99.

5   Backer, *op. cit.*, p. 159.

6   *Holy Bible*, New International Version, (Grand Rapids, Michigan: Zondervan Publishing House, 1984).

7   *Ibid.*

8   Elmore Leske, "In Memoriam," *British Lutheran* 21 (March/April1976), 2.

APPENDIX I

The Texts of the Hymns and Translations

A DIRECTORY

The Translations

The Original Hymns

APPENDIX II

The Hymns and Translations in Modern Hymnals

A GUIDE

KEY

ANH—*A New Hymnal for Colleges and Schools*
ANS—*A New Song*
CW—*Christian Worship: A Lutheran Hymnal*
EC—*Ecumenical Praise*
LBW—*Lutheran Book of Worship*
LW—*Lutheran Worship*
RTL—*Rejoice in the Lord*
TH82—*The Hymnal 1982*
TLH—*The Lutheran Hymnal*
UMH—*The United Methodist Hymnal*
WOR—*Worship*
WOR2—*Worship II*
WS—*Worship Supplement*

Translations

Isaiah in a Vision Did of Old: LBW 528
Rise Again, Ye Lion-Hearted: TLH 470
With High Delight Let Us Unite: WS 734, LBW 140, LW 134, CW 168

The Original Hymns

In Adam We Have All Been One: ANS 680, WS 759, WOR2 136, LBW 372, LW 292, CW 396
O Fearful Place, Where He Who Knows Our Heart: WS 774
O Kingly Love, That Faithfully: WS 757, LW 346, CW 335
O God, O Lord of Heaven and Earth: WS 759, WOR2 199, LBW 396, LW 319, CW 400

O Thou, Who Hast of Thy Pure Grace: WS 767, LBW 442, CW 407

Preach You the Word: LW 259, CW 544

Thy Strong Word Did Cleave the Darkness: WS 747, WOR2 280, LBW 233, LW 328, TH82 381, RTL 386, ANH 9 and 328, CW 280

Weary of All Trumpeting: WOR2 310, EP 113, TH82 572, UMH 442, ANH 526, CW 527

APPENDIX III

Examples of Franzmann's Early Poetry

The examples found in this appendix are taken from the *Black and Red*, the literary magazine of Northwestern College, Watertown, Wisconsin. The poems were printed in that magazine during the years 1922—1928 (volumes 26—31) when Martin Franzmann was a student at the Preparatory School and the College.

Autumn

A pleasant time, the year grown old,
Still has a boyish heart:
His cheeks are ruddy and his hair is gold.
He lingers smiling, as though loath to part.

The trees in gold and crimson gleam
Like castles in the fairy store
Of childhood years. The stream
Reflects their golden glory.

The corn stands in the shock;
The granary, the well filled bin,
And richly laden larder mock
The winter coming in.

(Vol. 26, no. 6, Nov. 1922, p. 154)

Heil'ge Nacht

Heil'ge Nacht! Die Glocken laeuten:
Ohne Dich waer'n wir verloren.
Heil'ge Nacht! Von allen Seiten
Hoert man: Gott ist Mensch geboren.

Heil'ge Nacht! Der Sterne Funkel
Leuchtet helle aus der Hoeh'
Und die Schatten, blaeulich dunkel,
Fallen zitternd auf den Schnee.

Heil'ge Nacht! Aus allen Huetten
Hoert man "Stille Nacht" erklingen.

Fromme Leut' nach frommen Sitten
Alte Weihnachtslieder singen.

Heil'ge Nacht! Auch in den Gassen
Freuen sich die Jung' und Alten.
Ueberall, auf Land und Strassen
Laesst Gott Fried' and Freude walten.

(Vol. 26, no. 7, Dec. 1922)

The Old and the New

Where are they now—the dreams, the hopes that made
    the last New Year seem bright and glorious?

With what high courage then entered we the lists.
And now, as round the old year softly fold the mists
Of dim forgottenness, how humbly do we leave them,
    dejected, unvictorious.

But see—another year, great gift of God, with promise
    large and manifold

Upon bright vistas of New Hope doth ope his portals
    wide,
And there upon the sea of Chance the ships of Promise
    ride
To bear us to the land of incense and of gold.

(Vol. 26, no. 8, Jan. 1923, p. 213)

To the Mississippi

When the sun is in the setting and the light is growing
    low
And the sedges sigh and whisper as the wind-breaths
    softly blow,
When the last rays of the sunset make the water flow-
    ing gold,
You are like a friendly father, like a true friend grow-
    ing old.

When the wild winds lash the waters and the clouds
    lay low above,
When the sedge-fowl seeks the shelter and the fisher-
    man the cove,

126

THY STRONG WORD

And when the thunders roar and lightening flashes
  sharp across the sky,
You are like an old man angered, like an anger mount-
  ing high.

When the soft gray light of morning, comes a stealing
  o'er the hill,
And the silvery water-ribbon lies all motionless and
  still,
You seem a child beginning this business called life,
Unacquainted yet with sorrow or with trouble or with
  strife.

Mississippi, king of rivers, almost human you appear
To one who lives beside you with an open eye and
  ear.
You are not mere flowing water, you're a quick and
  living thing
And the lapping of your waters has a human, friendly
  ring.

(Vol. 26, no. 9, Feb. 1923, p. 243)

Fruehlingstraum

In Traemen fuehl' ich schon den Hauch des Lenzes
  wehen.
In Traeumen seh' ich schon die Veilchen blueh'n.
Und wollig-weisse Wolken seh' ich am Himmel gehen;
Seh' Wald und Weide duftend, frisch und gruen.

Und ob mich schon die Winde rauh und kalt
  umblasen,
Sie hindern dennoch meine Traeume nicht.
Ich sehe nur die gruenen, blumenreichen Rasen,
Glitzernd mit Tau im frischen Morgenlicht.

Ich hoer' den Sang der Voegel wie aus weiter Ferne,
Ich fuehl' das Glueck der lauen Fruehlingsnacht,
Die Nacht von dunkelblauem Himmel, goldner Sterne—
So traeum' ich fort von holder Fruehlingspracht.

(Vol. 27, no. 1, April 1923, p. 1)

APPENDIX III

Beginning and End

Empires have lived and have flourished and have
    spread their dominions out wide;
Empires have lived and have flourished and are buried
    by time's cruel tide.
They were built up with towers that reached to the
    skies.
They spread their dominions, powerful, wise.
They covered the world with a network of roads;
Their ships came from far lands with rich, fragrant
    loads.

Their kings and the monarchs that ruled at their head
Their ashes are buried, silent and dead.
The towers they built are one with the earth.
Their ships in the sea have found a still berth.
But the songs they have sung and the words they have
    writ
On the tower of fame enthroned will sit

For the Empires that die are the birth of the Empires
    from the ruins that rise.
"The thing that is, it is that which shall be," spake
    Solomon, the mighty and wise.

(Vol. 27, no.1, April 1923, p. 1)

The Morn

I

The morn is crouching like a tawny pard
    Behind the hills of the East.
The leopard leaps—the dew on the sward
    Glitters, in splendor increased.
The morn, the leopard that crouches afar
    On the hills of the morning gray,
Arises and draws in the golden car
    Of the Lion-king of the day.

II

The willow trembles its dew-dripping tresses.
The flower its breast bares to the sun's warm caresses.
The mists rise like wraiths from the sun-sprinkled river.

128

THY STRONG WORD

The leaves like young birds in the morning wind
    quiver.
The rush of the river like the rippling of laughter
Sings the song of to-day that knows no hereafter.
The wind in the pine-trees with sound softly sonorous
Sings to God of the Morning in deer-reverent chorus.

III

Lord God of the morning, we praise thee, adore thee,
Our treasures, O master, we spread out before thee.
The soft, cool sand by the foam-flecked sea,
Father Creator, thy footstool shall be.
The odor of flowers from meadow and hill
As the incense we offer thy nostrils shall fill.
And in lands that are near and in lands that are far away
We will chorus thy glory, God of break of the day.

(Vol. 27, no. 3, June 1923, p. 66)

Day-Dreams

To see strange sights in distant lands,
Such sights as one can ne'er forget—
Graves royal wrought by million hands,
The mosques, bazaars, the minaret;
Eastern suns in fire that set;
Eastern drugs that dreams beget;
Cities where East and West have met.

In my good ship to sail away;
To cross wide space of surging seas;
To lounge upon the deck all day;
To feel the salty-wet sea breeze;
To sip my wine and take mine ease
On southern shores 'neath green palm trees.

Of such it is that dreams are made.
The world contains such things, 'tis said.
But I, I have not felt nor seen;
But for my dreams they had not been.

(Vol. 27, no. 6, Nov. 1923, p. 166)

APPENDIX III

A Railroad Carol

The snow is falling, falling slow
    And it's growing dark outside.
And the leagues of snow we still must go
    Are very, very wide.

The puffing engine chucks its way,
    Through windy, storm-swept miles.
Each heart is happiness today,
    And every face is smiles.

For weary miles mean nothing now,
    For rest we are going home.
Now rest in peace the tongues of Greece,
    And the languages of Rome.

I can hear the church bells ringing.
    I can hear happy children sing.
Sing on your happy singing.
    And ring, ye church bell, ring.

(Vol. 27, no. 7, Dec. 1923, p. 198)

Belshazzar

It was Babylon's king, grown fat in his pride,
Who gathered his lordlings from far and from wide,
And his wives and his concubines many and fair
At Babylon gathered to feast with him there.

And the vessels for which Nebuchadnezzar had fought,
From the temple of God to the banquet were brought
There the wining and dining and gay minstrelsy
And the fat king Belshazzar, full happy was he.
The lords all about and the king on his throne
Worshipped idols of brass and idols of stone.
And the gay king Belshazzar, with drinking grown
    bold,
Filled the cups of Jehovah of silver and gold.
Drunken he lolled on his dais of blue
And mockingly drank to the God of the Jew.

But the lords who applauded, as lordlings will,
And the shrill-laughing women grew suddenly still.

130

And the concubines, wives, and the lordlings all
Gazed on a Hand that wrote on the wall.
And the king, who was flushed as a leaf in October,
Gazed on the Hand and grew suddenly sober.
The brave King Belshazzar grew cold and afeared.
"Mene, Tekel, Upharsin"—the hand disappeared.
"Whoever shall read this writing for me,
The third in my mighty kingdom shall be!"
(The king's voice trembled brokenly
And trembled his hands as an aspen tree.)
He called his Chaldeans, his wise men all,
But none could decipher the script on the wall.

Then called he in Daniel, the prisoner Jew.
"And you are able, interpret this true."
Daniel spoke, and his voice had an echoing ring,
"Thou are weighed in the balance—found wanting, O
    King.
And thy kingdom and all that is subject to thee,
As God lives, the Medes' and the Persians' shall be."
That night, midst the thunder, lightning, and rain
Was Belshazzar, king of Chaldeans, slain.

(Vol. 27, no. 10, March 1924, p. 310)

Song for the Weary

Wait till the winter is over,
Wait till the springtime is come.
The bee will come home to the clover.
And peace to your hearts will come home.

When winds blow Araby spices,
And the river runs silver and blue,
You will find that a little suffices
To make your dreams come true.

Though the winter was sleety and dreary,
And love had little room,
Your heart will forget to be weary
When roses bloom.

(Vol. 28, no. 1, April 1924, p. 1)

APPENDIX III

When We Go Forth

Remember not our youthful sin,
    The follies we have gloried in.
Be with us still, as Thou hast been
    When we go forth.

And soften the regretful pain,
    The aching wish to do again.
Let us forget the hopes we've slain
    When we go forth.

Give Thou Thy peace into each heart
    That we may play the manly part.
And with Thy blessing bid us start
    When we go forth.

What's done, or well, or ill, is done,
    But in what is to be begun
We look to Thee, almighty One,
    When we go forth.

(Vol. 28, no. 3, June 1924, p. 61)

October

When the gay lights of autumn are golden and red,
And the sun rises late and goes early to bed,
When the blackbirds wheel southward and swoop o'er
    the corn,
When the blue mists of autumn blur the hill-tops at
    morn,
When the wind has a touch of the winter to come,
My heart feels a longing for the lamplights of home.

In the grateful dusk of the late afternoon,
In the calm, golden shower of the late harvest moon,
In the great starlit glory of cold, silent night,
When the poplar-leaves quiver with silvery delight,
In the smell of the earth of freshly turned loam,
My heart feels the call of the prairie and home.

(Vol. 28, no. 5, October 1924, p. 127)

THY STRONG WORD

Christmas

We all remember them, those early Christmas days,
When bells ring out with simple, loving lays,
And Christmas nights when, as the church bells cease,
The after-ring hangs like an incense, bearing peace.

The sun glints diamond-patterned in the snow,
The lean trees shiver, creaking to and fro,
The hard-packed snowpaths crunch neath passing feet,
And all is coldly bright and clear and sweet;
And from the latticed steeple-lofts the church bells say

> Christ was born,
> Christ was born,
> Christ was born today.

The moon cuts slanting cold-blue shadows on the
    white
Lying in drifted peace this Holy Night.
The lights of home gleam golden through the dark,
Against the moon the elms stand gauntly stark;
And from the church bells spell out again,

> Peace on earth,
> Peace on earth,
> Peace on earth, good will toward men.

Those olden, childhood Christmas days are past;
But through the march of striding years their song will
    last,
Ringing their olden peaceful message down
Faintly, as lights shine from a valley town,
Those silver mellow bells that say

> Christ was born,
> Christ was born,
> Christ was born today.

(Vol. 28, no. 7, December 1924, pp. 187—188)

A Sonnet

Now Autumn, silent, stalks with pensive pace
Upon brown woodlands and the weary field,
Bringing last glory sun and frost can yield

Before chaste Winter's simple, clean-cut grace.
The whirling west wind cannot yet efface
The glory that was Summer that was Spring,
The brown field silently remembering
The beauty of its tender lush-green space.

There is a solitude in Autumn's breath,
A poignant loneliness beyond recall,
A somber peace beyond all reckoning.
This dying-off is but a transient death,
And hope is bright in garish leaves that fall:
For this is travail that shall bring forth Spring.

(Vol. 29, no. 6, November 1925, p. 181)

River Dam, Mississippi

O you, who from the headsprings of the north
In youthful gloriousness came pouring forth,
Where endlessly the aisles of pine-trees stand
In green solemnity on either hand,
Who in the youthful, headstrong pride you bore
Have whipped the slender willows on your shore,
Generous of breadth and sinuous in length,
Exulting in your rapid, northborn strength
Compacted of the wilderness of your home
In long, free arabesques of flood and foam
O river, must you pause and fall,
Over this human, concrete wall,
In humble passiveness slide through
These great machines that sinews drew
And lose the lusty glory of your pride
To pass so limpid on the other side?
Could you not smash this human gate
With all the strength of pent-up hate,
Scatter the walls, the shafts, the cranks
In huge confusion on your banks
On rush with roaring melody
Forever and forever to the sea?

(Vol. 29, no. 9, February 1926, p. 284)

THY STRONG WORD

Vale Pick and Shovel

Farewell smell of fresh-dug clay,
Sweeter than the much-sung hay,
Farewell empty streets and lots,
Farewell Polish patriots,
Farewell muscles taut and tough,
Farewell dirty hands and rough,
Farewell sun and Godsent breeze
(In varying proportions, these),
Farewell labor grim and dour—
And farewell sixty cents an hour.

(Vol. 30, no. 4, September 1926, p. 119)

Three Green Candles—

Three green candles, burning fair,
A polished floor, a curving stair,
A fragile table, vase of jade,
And, gleaming dully where it hung,
Splashed upon a silk sarong,
One gilt dragon in the shade—
The three green candles, on the floor,
Made golden pathways to the door.
The table cast off bits of light;
The vase shown greenly in the night;
The gilted dragon dreamt of seas
In other lands and centuries.

It was some subtle sort of sin,
Alert for me to enter in.

(Vol. 30, no. 5, October 1926, p. 150)

Who Weds a Goddess

Who weds a goddess
His feet shall be swift
For treading cloudlands
And sunsets-rift.

Who weds a goddess,
Again and again

APPENDIX III

His ears shall be quickened
For the beauty of rain.

Who weds a goddess,
His feet shall be swift—
Shall have pain for a dowry
And tears for a gift.

(Vol. 30, no. 7, December 1926, p. 218)

Return

I've been adrift on parlous, surging seas,
On seas no man has dared to sail before,
Piratic half-breed or conquistador.
My keel has foundered where the oceans freeze
And drifted where the torpid tropic breeze
Lulls man to deep forgetting evermore,
Where lotus blooms, and jungle-creatures roar;
Mid stranger seas and sights more strange than these.

And now, all safe within this harbor wall,
Where comes no storm, where everlasting peace
Falls like a benediction over all,
Beyond the bar I hear the sea-winds call,
Wildly, bewitchingly without surcease:
I've followed once, and once shall be my all.

(Vol. 30, no. 9, February 1927, p. 316)

Hellas

O land of Homer, Sophocles,
Of Hesiod, Euripides,
Alcaeus, Sappho, Heracles,
And some not quite as great as these—
That haptly you might light upon
In Weltgeschichte, Volume One—
But as I said, O Grecian land,
I find it hard to understand
How men could find the time to play,
To rest, and pass the time of day
And love, and dance, and drink their wine,
Or even take time out to dine,

When every time they wish to say
Some commonplace the proper way,
They had to page all through and through
Kaegi One or Kaegi Two.

(Vol. 31, no. 2, May 1927, p. 37)

Apology for Greek Syntax

Of many roads that lead to Troy,
Where Helen is, where every one
That e'er had dreamings, man or boy,

Deems his life shall have begun,
I know of none that brings much joy,
That knows not storms and heat and sun,

Cold nights and sirens to decoy
And mountain tops scarce to be won
And dragons waiting to destroy.

But of them all that have begun
Their journey on that road to Troy,
Until these headlands shall be won,
Until they have the golden fleece
There's not a man of them will cease.

(Vol. 31, no. 6, November 1927, p. 169)

To Any Genius

Whatever plodding steps we take,
Whatever weary ways we run,
We shall be ever in your wake,
You shall be nearer to the sun.

Whatever pleasant sights we see,
Whatever of delight be ours,
You shall see greater sights than we
And have more spans of wreathed hours.

But while we gather jovially
Around some half-way marking stone,
Upon the hilltop eminently
You shall be very much alone.

(Vol. 31, no. 10, March 1928, p. 303)

BIBLIOGRAPHY

Primary Sources

Black and Red. Vol. 26–31, November 1922–March 1928.

Franzmann, Alice B. Correspondence. October 1991, January 1992,September 1992.

Franzmann, Gerhardt. Correspondence. May 1992.

Franzmann, John W. "Westfield's Window." *British Lutheran* (June–July 1971): 9.

Franzmann, Martin H. "A Sonnet." *Black and Red* 29, no. 6 (November 1928): 181.

_____, "Augustana II: Of Original Sin." *Concordia Theological Monthly* 20, no. 12 (December 1949): 885.

_____, "Christ, the Hope of Glory." *Concordia Theological Monthly* 24, no. 12 (December 1953): 900.

_____, *Christian Hymns* (some translations). St. Peter's Lutheran Church, Cleveland, Ohio, 1934.

_____, "Christian Poetry." *Northwestern Lutheran* 33 (1946): 134, 154, 172, 182.

_____, *Ha! Ha! Among the Trumpets.* St. Louis: Concordia Publishing House, 1966.

_____, "Heil'ge Nacht." *Black and Red* 26, no. 7 (December 1922): 180.

_____, "Of a Man and Four Rivers." *British Lutheran* 14, no. 8 (October 1969): 6.

_____, "Quick and Powerful." *Concordia Theological Monthly* 22, no. 3 (March 1951): 164ff.

_____, "To the Mississippi." *Black and Red* 26, no. 9 (February 1923).

_____, "The Last Look." *British Lutheran* 16, no. 2 (November–December 1971): 2.

_____, "Theological Conferences in Europe, Summer 1956." *Lutheran Witness* 75 (September 25, 1956): 370.

_____, "Why So Many Bibles?" *Lutheran Witness* 81 (March 20,1962): 134ff.

Franzmann, Peter B. Interview. August 1992.

Franzmann, Werner. Interviews. May 1992, July 1992.

Franzmann, William. Interview. May 1992.

Heinitz, Kenneth L. (a former student of Martin Franzmann). Conversation. November 1992.

Katt, Helen Franzmann. Interview. July 1992.

_____, "Our Singing Mother." Orlando, Florida, 1977.

Schindler, Walter. Interview. June 1992.

Secondary Sources

Books

Backer, Bruce. *Lutheran Worship: A Course Guide.* 4th ed. New Ulm, Minnesota: Luther College, 1988.

Companion to Lutheran Book of Worship, Minneapolis: Augsburg Publishing House, 1981.

Holy Bible. New International Version. Grand Rapids, Michigan: Zondervan Publishing House, 1984.

Katt, Arthur F. *Critical Comments on the Proposed New Hymnal,* Shaker Heights, Ohio: July 15–September 15, 1939.

Koch, John B. *When the Murray Meets the Mississippi,* North Adelaide, South Australia: Lutheran Publishing House of South Australia, 1975.

Lutheran Worship Hymnal Companion, St. Louis: Concordia Publishing House, 1992.

Polack, W. G. *The Handbook of the Lutheran Hymnal.* 3rd ed. St.Louis: Concordia Publishing House, 1958.

Magazine Articles

Bartling, Victor A. "A Martin Franzmann Bibliography." *Concordia Theological Monthly* 43, no. 6 (June 1972): 485.

Fuerbringer, Alfred O. and Franzmann, Martin H. "A Quarter Century of Interchurch Relations: 1935–1960." *Concordia Theological Monthly* 32, no. 1 (January 1962): 5.

_____, "Reports on Interchurch Relations." *Concordia Theological Monthly* 33, no. 1 (January 1962): 5.

Friedrich, E. J. "They Studied Christian Doctrine." *Lutheran Witness* 79: 538.

Jungkuntz, Richard. "Editorial." *Concordia Theological Monthly* 43, no. 6 (June 1972).

Koening, Paul. "Free Conference in Europe." *Lutheran Witness* 72, no. 19 (September 15, 1953): 319.

Korby, Kenneth F. "Notes From the Editor's Notebook." *The Cresset* 40 (November–December 1976): 4–5.

Leske, Elmore. "In Memoriam." *British Lutheran* 21 (March–April 1976): 2.

"Light from Above." *The Lutheran Witness* 73, no. 22 (October 26, 1954): 2.

"News from Concordia Seminary." *Lutheran Witness* 65, no. 25 (December 1946): 410.

Redlin, G. "Obituary for Rev. William Franzmann." *Northwestern Lutheran* 26, no. 18 (December 27, 1953).

Rutz, Karl. "Ha! Ha! Among the Trumpets." *Response* 17, no. 1 (1977).

The Lutheran Witness, "An obituary for Martin Hans Franzmann." Summer 1976.

Webber, F. R. "The Fine Arts in the Service of the Church." *American Lutheran* 20, no. 6 (June 1937): 9.

"Westfield Begins Academic Year with New Tutor." *British Lutheran* 14, no. 8 (October 1969): 8.

Bulletins

Bulletin. "The Installation Service of Dr. Martin H.Franzmann, D.D. as Theological Tutor of Westfield House." Abbey Church, Cambridge, England, October 4, 1969.

Bulletin. "The Memorial Service, Martin Hans Oscar Franzmann." Abbey Church, Cambridge, England, April 12, 1976.

Memorial Service Bulletin for Martin Franzmann. Concordia Seminary, St. Louis, Missouri, April 2, 1976.

Service Folder. "A Service of Praise and Thanksgiving Celebrating 40 Years in the Pastoral Ministry of The Reverend Carl A.Gaertner, D.D." Zion Lutheran Church, Dallas, Texas, September 29, 1974.

Hymnals

A New Hymnal for Colleges and Schools, New Haven and London: Yale University Press, 1992.

A New Song. St. Louis: Concordia Publishing House, 1967.

Ecumenical Praise, Carol Stream, Illinois: Agape Publishing (a division of Hope Publishing), 1977.

Hymnal 1982. New York: The Church Hymnal Corporation, 1985.

Lutheran Book of Worship, Minneapolis, Minnesota: Augsburg Publishing House, 1978.

Lutheran Worship, St. Louis: Concordia Publishing House, 1982.

Rejoice in the Lord, ed. Erik Routley. Grand Rapids, Michigan: Eerdmans Publishing Company, 1985.

The Lutheran Hymnal, St. Louis: Concordia Publishing House, 1941.

The United Methodist Hymnal, Nashville, Tennessee: The United Methodist Press, 1989.

Worship, Chicago: G.I.A. Publications, Inc., 1971.

Worship II, Chicago: G.I.A. Publications, Inc., 1975.

Worship Supplement, St. Louis: Concordia Publishing House, 1969.

Other Papers

Klatt, Dennis. *The Brothers Franzmann: A Strengthening Influence on the Bible-Based Theology of the Wisconsin Synod,*Watertown, Wisconsin: Northwestern College, 1988.

BV 330 .F65 B75 1993
Brinkley, Richard N.
Thy strong word

BV 330 .F65 B75 1993
Brinkley, Richard N.
Thy strong word

DATE	ISSUED TO
JUL 25 '94	R. Schmidt

CONCORDIA COLLEGE LIBRARY
2811 NE Holman St.
Portland, OR 97211